WHEN THE HEAVEN SPLITS

A concise and comprehensive commentary of Sūrah Inshiqāq, Sūrah Burūj, Sūrah Tāriq, Sūrah A'lā which discusses the incidents of Judgement Day and how we can make preparation for this inevitable Day.

By
Shaykh Mufti Saiful Islām

Published in December 2018
ISBN: 978-1-909114-34-0
British Library Cataloguing in Publication Data
A catalogue record for this book is available from the British Library.

Publisher's Note:

Every care and attention has been put into the production of this book. If however, you find any errors, they are our own, for which we seek Allāh's ﷻ forgiveness and the reader's pardon.

Published by:

JKN Publications
118 Manningham Lane
Bradford
West Yorkshire
BD8 7JF
United Kingdom

t: +44 (0) 1274 308 456 | w: www.jkn.org.uk | e: info@jkn.org.uk

Book Title: When the Heaven Splits

Author: Shaykh Mufti Saiful Islām

Printed by Mega Printing in Turkey

"In the Name of Allāh, the Most Beneficent,
the Most Merciful"

Contents

Contents

Introduction

All praises belong to Allāh 🕮 and may His peace, salutations and blessings be upon the final Messenger, Muhammad 🕮, upon his noble Sahābahs 🕮, Tābi'īn and those who follow their noble path until the Day of Judgement. Āmīn!

This book contains the commentary of four Sūrahs from Juzz Amma namely; Sūrah Inshiqāq, Sūrah Burūj, Sūrah Tāriq and Sūrah A'lā. The first two Sūrahs contain a common theme of capturing the scenes and events of the Last Day and how this world will come to an end. However, all four Sūrahs mentioned, have a connection of the journey of humanity, reflection on nature, how nature changes and most importantly, giving severe warnings to mankind about the punishments and exhorting them to prepare for the Hereafter through good deeds and refraining from sins. Sūrah Burūj, Sūrah Tāriq take oath in the creation of Allāh 🕮 to express the importance of certain things so that mankind remind themselves of the destruction that will occur during the end of the world.

In this book, my beloved teacher and Shaykh, Shaykh Mufti Saiful Islām Sāhib has summarised the vast commentaries that are available of these four Sūrahs to make it easy to understand for people of all ages.

May Allāh ﷻ protect us from the hardships and torments of that Final Day! May Allāh ﷻ accept the efforts of all those who have participated in the writing and compilation of this book, especially my beloved teacher and Shaykh, Mufti Saiful Islām Sāhib and reward them in the life of this world and the Hereafter. Āmīn!

Maulāna **Ismāīl** *Azīz*
Graduate of JKN
September 2018 / Dhul-Hijjah 1439

Sūrah Inshiqāq
The Splitting
Revealed in Makkah

بِسْمِ اللهِ الرَّحْمٰنِ الرَّحِيْمِ

In the Name of Allāh, the Most Compassionate, the Most Merciful

إِذَا السَّمَآءُ انْشَقَّتْ . وَأَذِنَتْ لِرَبِّهَا وَحُقَّتْ . وَإِذَا الْأَرْضُ مُدَّتْ . وَأَلْقَتْ مَا فِيهَا وَتَخَلَّتْ . وَأَذِنَتْ لِرَبِّهَا وَحُقَّتْ

1. When the sky will split apart.
2. and will listen to its Lord, and it ought to.
3. and When the earth will be stretched out
4. and it will throw up whatever it contains and will become empty.
5. It will listen to its Lord, and it ought to.

Horrors of Judgement Day
Verse 1

إِذَا السَّمَآءُ انْشَقَّتْ

When the sky will split apart.

Allāh ﷻ commences Sūrah Inshiqāq by speaking about the conditionsof the sky and the earth on the Day of Judgement.

8

All dead bodies shall resurrect altogether and the earth will disclose its treasures. Just like the sky, the earth will listen to its Lord as it rightly should. Both the sky and the earth are obliged to obey Allāh's ﷻ command and do what He wants them to do.

These opening five verses of the Sūrah is the شَرْط (Shart) condition and the جَزَاء (Jazā—result of the consequence—which is the hidden clause, **"On that Day, men will see the deeds he committed."**

Allāh ﷻ says in Sūrah Ibrāhīm,

$$\text{يَوْمَ تُبَدَّلُ الْأَرْضُ غَيْرَ الْأَرْضِ وَالسَّمَاوَاتُ}$$

"The Day when the earth will be changed into another earth, and the skies will also be changed." (14:48)

People will then be called to account for their actions as they stand on an earth completely different from the earth we know.

$$\text{وَبَرَزُوا اِللّٰهِ الْوَاحِدِ الْقَهَّارِ}$$

"They will then present themselves before Allāh, the One, the Most Dominant." (14:48)

Two types of Commands

Verse 2:

وَأَذِنَتْ لِرَبِّهَا وَحُقَّتْ

"The sky will listen to the command of its Lord, and it ought to."

The verb, أَذِنَتْ means it will listen. Here listening includes obedience. The verb, حُقَّتُ may be interpreted as, it had an obligation to listen and obey Allāh's ﷻ command.

Divine Commands are of two types,

1. Divinely legislated (Tashrī'ī) Commands
2. Destined (Takwīnī) Commands

The first type, Tashrī'ī commands, the command appears as a law and violation of it is punishable. Mankind and Jinn are not forced in the sense that they become unable to violate it. Instead, they both have their free will to choose whether to abide by the law or to violate it. Such laws are imposed upon those who are endowed with intellect like humans and Jinn. This divides them into believers and non-believers, obedient and disobedient. In the second type (اَحْكَامُ تَكْوِينِيْ) Destined Command, there is no free will at all. The entire universe including humans and Jinn are unable to act contrary to this type of command.

In Sūrah Hā Mīm Sajdah, Allāh ﷻ addressing the heavens and the earth says,

اِئْتِيَا طَوْعًا أَوْ كَرْهًا قَالَتَا أَتَيْنَا طَائِعِينَ

"Come to Us (submit to Us) willingly or unwillingly." Both replied, "We shall come willingly." (41:11)

The Destined Command is also made reference to in the verse of Sūrah Al-Imrān where Allāh ﷻ reprimands those who turn away from the pledge."

"Do they (those who turn away from the pledge) seek a Dīn besides the Dīn of Allāh (the Dīn of Islām) when all within the heavens and the earth willingly or unwillingly surrender to Him and (when it is) to Him (that) they will all be returned (for reckoning on the Day of Judgement)." (3:83)

Verse 3:

وَإِذَا الْأَرْضُ مُدَّتْ

And when the earth will be stretched

The word, مُدَّ (Mudda) means to stretch, spread, expand out. This is so to give room for the creation to assemble.

Sayyidunā Jābir ؓ narrates that the Holy Prophet ﷺ said, "On the Day of Judgement, the earth will be stretched out like leather (or rubber) and expanded into a flat plain allowing enough space on it for the entire human race to keep their feet."

To understand this Hadīth, it must be remembered that on the Day of Judgement, the entire mankind from the beginning of creation untill resurrection will be brought back to life simultaneously. Thus, each individual will have just enough space on the earth where he could place his feet.

Verse 4:

وَأَلْقَتْ مَا فِيْهَا وَتَخَلَّتْ

And it will throw up whatever it contains and will become empty.

The earth will with one convulsion cast out whatever it contained in its inner soil such as its natural treasures or buried treasures, mines, dead human bodies and their remains and particles.

Allāh ﷻ mentions the same points in Sūrah Zilzāl- The Convulsion.

إِذَا زُلْزِلَتِ الْأَرْضُ زِلْزَالَهَا . وَأَخْرَجَتِ الْأَرْضُ أَثْقَالَهَا . وَقَالَ الْإِنْسَانُ مَا لَهَا . يَوْمَئِذٍ تُحَدِّثُ أَخْبَارَهَا . بِأَنَّ رَبَّكَ أَوْحَى لَهَا .

"When the earth shall quake most violently (shake with a quake), when the earth will throw up loads of dead bodies and treasures, man will ask, "What is the matter with her (why is the earth doing this)?" On that Day, she (the earth) will narrate her accounts (by giving evidence against people because she would have seen everything that had been done on her), the earth will do this because your Lord will command her to do so." (99:1-5)

Here again, the command is تَكْوِينِيّ, Destined Command to the earth.

يَا أَيُّهَا الْإِنْسَانُ إِنَّكَ كَادِحٌ إِلَى رَبِّكَ كَدْحًا فَمُلَاقِيهِ . فَأَمَّا مَنْ أُوتِيَ كِتَابَهُ بِيَمِينِهِ . فَسَوْفَ يُحَاسَبُ حِسَابًا يَّسِيرًا . وَيَنْقَلِبُ إِلَى أَهْلِهِ مَسْرُورًا . وَأَمَّا مَنْ أُوتِيَ كِتَابَهُ وَرَاءَ ظَهْرِهِ . فَسَوْفَ يَدْعُوْ ثُبُورًا . وَّيَصْلَى سَعِيْرًا . إِنَّهُ كَانَ فِي أَهْلِهِ مَسْرُورًا . إِنَّهُ ظَنَّ أَنْ لَّنْ يَّحُورَ . بَلَى إِنَّ رَبَّهُ كَانَ بِهِ بَصِيرًا

6. O Mankind! Indeed you make great efforts in your journey towards your Lord and will soon meet with (the fruit of) your effort.

7. As for him who is given his record in his right hand,

8. an easy reckoning will be taken from him

9. and he will return happily to his family.

10. As for him who is given his record behind his back,

11. he will soon call for destruction

12. and will enter the blazing fire.

13. Indeed! he used to be happy among his family.

14. He used to think that he would not return.

15. Why not! Verily his Lord was ever watchful over him.

Man's Life
Verse 6:

يَا أَيُّهَا الْإِنسَانُ إِنَّكَ كَادِحٌ إِلَىٰ رَبِّكَ كَدْحًا فَمُلَاقِيهِ

O' mankind, Indeed you make great efforts in your journey to-wards your Lord and will soon meet (the fruit of) your efforts.

This verse summarises man's life in this world. Everything that a person needs in this world requires some effort from him and everything that man says or does in this effort are recorded. The world is fast in this manner and the Day of Judgement is approaching near. In fact, every person's individual Qiyāmah starts when he passes away. Eventually, the trumpet or the bugle will be sounded and everything will cease to exist.

Return to Allāh ﷻ

In Abū Dāwūd At-Tayālisi, a Hadīth has been related by Sayyidunā Jābir ؓ that the Holy Prophet ﷺ said,

Sayyidunā Jibrīl ؑ said, "O' Muhammad! Live how you wish, for verily you will die; love what you wish, for verily you will part with it, and do what you wish, for verily you will meet it (your deed)". (Abū Dāwūd At-Tayālisi).

Mankind is addressed in this verse and shown a road that were he to ponder carefully and use his senses and intelligence properly, he would exert all his effort in the right direction to secure his well-being and safety in this world as well as in the Hereafter. First, it has been pointed out that man, whether he is good or bad, believer or non-believer, has the natural tendency to use his hard efforts towards achieving his goal. A good-natured person will work hard and adopt lawful means to acquire his livelihood and necessities of life. A bad person cannot obtain his needs and objective without working hard. Even thieves, robbers, cheaters and looters use their deficient intelligence and physical strength to achieve their objectives.

Secondly, after death he must give into account his deeds and his efforts. This is necessary and logistic so that the consequences of his good and bad actions become apparent since they are not known in this life. An upright person may work hard for months on end in order to obtain his livelihood and necessities of life, but thieves and looters may obtain them overnight. Were there not to be any form of reckoning or punishment, both of them (the good and the bad) will be equal, which is contrary to reason and justice.

Reckoning in front of Allāh ﷻ
Verses 7-9

فَأَمَّا مَنْ أُوتِيَ كِتَابَهُ بِيَمِينِهِ . فَسَوْفَ يُحَاسَبُ حِسَابًا يَسِيرًا . وَيَنْقَلِبُ إِلَى أَهْلِهِ مَسْرُورًا

**As for him who is given his record in his right hand,
an easy reckoning will be taken from him, and he will return
happily to his family.**

When the trumpet is blown for the second time, people will emerge from their graves and present themselves before Allāh ﷻ

for reckoning. The records of deeds will then be distributed among mankind.

Allāh ﷻ says,

"As for him who is given his record in his right hand, an easy reckoning will be taken from him and he will return happily to his family." (84:7-9)

Allāh ﷻ says in Sūrah Ḥāqqa,

فَأَمَّا مَنْ أُوتِيَ كِتَابَهُ بِيَمِينِهِ فَيَقُولُ هَاؤُمُ اقْرَءُوا كِتَابِيَهْ . إِنِّي ظَنَنْتُ أَنِّي مُلَاقٍ حِسَابِيَهْ .
فَهُوَ فِي عِيشَةٍ رَّاضِيَةٍ . فِي جَنَّةٍ عَالِيَةٍ . قُطُوفُهَا دَانِيَةٌ . كُلُوا وَاشْرَبُوا هَنِيئًا بِمَا أَسْلَفْتُمْ فِي
الْأَيَّامِ الْخَالِيَةِ

"As for the one who receives his reward (of deeds) in his right hand, he will call out, "Come and read my record! I was always convinced that I shall certainly meet my reckoning." So he will enjoy a pleasing life in lofty gardens. The fruit of these gardens are near at hand. (They will be told), "Eat and drink with all blessings as a reward for the (good) deeds that you sent ahead during the days bygone." (69:19-24)

Imām Aḥmad ﷺ reports from Sayyidah Āishah ﷺ that the Holy Prophet ﷺ said, "Whoever is interrogated during the reckoning, then he will be punished. Sayyidah Āishah ﷺ then said, "But didn't Allāh ﷺ say,

فَسَوْفَ يُحَاسَبُ حِسَابًا يَّسِيْرًا

"He surely will receive an easy reckoning."

The Holy Prophet ﷺ replied, "That is not referring to the reckoning, rather it is referring to the presentation. Whoever is interrogated during the reckoning on the Day of Judgement, then he will be punished." (Bukhāri, Muslim, Tirmizi)

This explanation of the Holy Prophet ﷺ clarifies that the deeds of the believers will also be presented before Allāh ﷻ, but by virtue of their faith not all of their actions will be scrutinised. This is referred to receiving an account in an easy manner.

The words, **"He will go back to his people joyfully,"** can be interpreted in one of two ways. This may refer to the Hūrs who will be his family members in Paradise, or it may refer to his family members in the world who will be present at the Plain of Resurrection, and he after knowing about his success will impart to them, according to the custom of this life, the welcoming news of his achievement. On the other hand, as for he who is given his record behind his back, he will soon call for destruction and will enter the Blazing Fire.

Allāh ﷻ mentions in Sūrah Hāqqa that these people will receive their records of deeds in their left hands. These will be given to them from behind their backs. This will be when every person shall see the fruits of his efforts.

Such people are described in the following verses in Sūrah Hāqqa, Allāh ﷺ says,

وَأَمَّا مَنْ أُوتِيَ كِتَابَهُ بِشِمَالِهِ فَيَقُولُ يَا لَيْتَنِي لَمْ أُوتَ كِتَابِيَهْ . وَلَمْ أَدْرِ مَا حِسَابِيَهْ. يَا لَيْتَهَا كَانَتِ الْقَاضِيَةَ

"As for the one who receives his record in the left hand, he will cry. 'Oh dear, if only I were not given my record and I had not known any reckoning! Alas! If only death had been my end'".
(69:25-27)

Plight of the Disbelievers
Verses 10-13

وَأَمَّا مَنْ أُوتِيَ كِتَابَهُ وَرَاءَ ظَهْرِهِ. فَسَوْفَ يَدْعُو ثُبُورًا . وَيَصْلَى سَعِيرًا . إِنَّهُ كَانَ فِي أَهْلِهِ مَسْرُورًا

As for him who is given his record behind his back, he will soon call for destruction, and will enter the blazing fire. Indeed! he used to be happy among his family.

Allāh ﷺ describing the horrific scenes of Jahannam says,

مِنْ وَرَائِهِ جَهَنَّمُ وَيُسْقَى مِنْ مَّاءٍ صَدِيدٍ . يَتَجَرَّعُهُ وَلَا يَكَادُ يُسِيغُهُ وَيَأْتِيهِ الْمَوْتُ مِنْ كُلِّ مَكَانٍ وَّمَا هُوَ بِمَيِّتٍ وَمِنْ وَّرَائِهِ عَذَابٌ غَلِيظٌ

"Before him (waiting for the disbeliever in the Hereafter) is Jahannam, where he will be given (oozing) pus to drink. He will drink it (because of the extreme thirst) gulping (not all at once because of its terrible taste and odour) and it will not go down his throat. (The causes of) Death will come to him from all sides, but he will not die (because there is no death in the Hereafter). (This will not be the end because) before him (still to come) will be (even more) severe punishment (head to toe)." (14:16-17)

Shaykhul Islām Allāmah Shabbīr Ahmad Uthmāni ﷺ under these verses writes that it means they will not drink it happily and readily. It is mentioned in the Hadīth that the Angels will forcibly pour it down their throats after hammering them. When they will bring it near the mouth, the skin of the brain will hang down due to intense heat, after entering it into the mouth, it will stick to the throat. With great pain and difficulty they will swallow the liquid pus (down the throat) in gulps. No sooner will it reach their stomach that their intestines will come out of the stomach.

Allāh ﷺ says in another place,

وَإِن يَّسْتَغِيثُوا يُغَاثُوا بِمَآءٍ كَالْمُهْلِ يَشْوِي الْوُجُوهَ بِئْسَ الشَّرَابُ وَسَآءَتْ مُرْتَفَقًا

"If they plead for help, they will be helped with water that is like the remains of burnt oil (boiling and black), which will scorch their faces. A terrible drink indeed (which will be of no help at all to them)! It (Jahannam) is the worst of resting places (because it offers no rest at all)." (18:29)

Shaykhul Islām, further on says, "Its drinking would indeed be a confrontation with death. From head to toe, the pangs of death would fall on every limb of the body, from six sides the fatal chastisement shall attack. They will prefer death over this life, but death will not come to cease these extreme pains. Fresh and new chastisement and punishment will follow."

كُلَّمَا نَضِجَتْ جُلُوْدُهُمْ بَدَّلْنَاهُمْ جُلُوْدًا غَيْرَهَا لِيَذُوْقُوا الْعَذَابَ

"Whenever their skins roast (is burnt up in Jahannam), We shall exchange them for (replace them with) fresh skins so that they may taste the (full extent of the continuous) punishment." (4:56)

In another place, Allāh ﷺ says,

ثُمَّ لَا يَمُوْتُ فِيْهَا وَلَا يَحْيٰى

"Then (when he enters Jahannam) he will neither die there (and will therefore suffer forever) nor live (a life worth living)."(87:13)

A poet has truly said,

"Now they say out of frustration, 'We will die.' After dying, they could not find any solace, so where will they flee now."
May Allāh ﷺ save us. Āmīn.

Allāh ﷺ explaining Jahannam in another place, mentions the humiliating plight of the disbelievers;

إِذَا رَأَتْهُمْ مِّن مَّكَانٍ بَعِيدٍ سَمِعُوا لَهَا تَغَيُّظًا وَزَفِيرًا . وَإِذَا أُلْقُوا مِنْهَا مَكَانًا ضَيِّقًا مُقَرَّنِينَ

دَعَوْا هُنَالِكَ ثُبُورًا . لَا تَدْعُوا الْيَوْمَ ثُبُورًا وَّاحِدًا وَّادْعُوا ثُبُورًا كَثِيرًا .

**"When it (Jahannam) will see them from a distance (on the Day
of Judgement), (it will be so intense that) they will hear its fury
and its crackling (flames). When they are flung into a narrow
place (in Jahannam) with their hands and feet in shackles, they
will cry out for destruction (they will plead for death) to come to
them. (However, they will be told) "Do not cry for only one
destruction (death) today, but cry for many a destruction
regardless of how much you wish for it, death will never come
to you and you will suffer here forever)." (25:12-14)**

Indeed in the world, he used to be happy among his family. He
used to enjoy himself in the world without any concern for the
Day of Judgement. In addition to this, he used to think that he
would not return to account for his deeds before Allāh ﷻ. However, his belief was false. Allāh ﷻ declares, "He certainly will have to
return to Allāh ﷻ to account for his deeds. He was wrong to think
that Allāh ﷻ was unaware of his deeds because verily his Lord
was ever Watchful over him."

Rewards for the Believers

The true believers on the other hand are never oblivious of the
Hereafter, not even for a moment in this world. They are always
anxious and worried about the Hereafter during every pleasurable
moments.

In Sūrah Tūr, Allāh ﷻ quotes the saying of the true believers when they will enter Paradise.

وَأَقْبَلَ بَعْضُهُمْ عَلَىٰ بَعْضٍ يَتَسَآءَلُونَ . قَالُوٓا إِنَّا كُنَّا قَبْلُ فِىٓ أَهْلِنَا مُشْفِقِينَ . فَمَنَّ اللهُ عَلَيْنَا

وَوَقَانَا عَذَابَ السَّمُومِ . إِنَّا كُنَّا مِن قَبْلُ نَدْعُوهُ إِنَّهُ هُوَ الْبَرُّ الرَّحِيمُ

"They (the people of Jannah) will face each other asking questions. They will say, "Before this (in the world) we used to be fearful (of Jahannam) among our families (houses). However, Allāh favoured us and saved us from the punishment of the scorching wind (of Jahannam). Indeed, before this (in the world) we always used to pray (call) to Him to save us from Jahannam. Allāh answered our prayers because He is certainly the One Who treats with kindness, the Most Merciful." (52:25-28)

In other words, they enjoyed their moments with their families and yet were fearful and conscious of the Hereafter. The consequences of these two groups shall accord with their respective status. Those who led a life of luxury in this world with their families whilst being oblivious of the Hereafter will be punished in the next world. Those who were conscious of the Day of Reckoning will live with their families in eternal luxury and happiness in the next life.

This indicates that a true believer should not be immersed in the comfort of this worldly life. Under no circumstance should a believer be oblivious to the reckoning of the Hereafter. How beautifully our beloved Prophet ﷺ said, "Beware of living luxuriously, for the true servants of Allāh ﷻ do not live luxuriously." (Ahmad)

Verse 14

إِنَّه ظَنَّ أَنْ لَنْ يَّحُوْرَ

He used to think that he would not return.

Regarding the word لَنْ يَّحُوْرَ, in the verse 14, **"They would not return,"** Sayyidunā Abdullāh Ibn Abbās ؓ says,
"I did not recognise and understand the Tafsīr of it until I heard a Bedouin woman saying to her daughter, Hūri—i.e. come back.

Subhān-Allāh—The Mufassir of this Ummah takes knowledge from an ordinary Bedouin woman. May Allāh ﷻ bless us with the true knowledge of Dīn. Amīn!

فَلَا أُقْسِمُ بِالشَّفَقِ . وَاللَّيْلِ وَمَا وَسَقَ . وَالْقَمَرِ إِذَا اتَّسَقَ . لَتَرْكَبُنَّ طَبَقًا عَنْ طَبَقٍ . فَمَا لَهُمْ لَا يُؤْمِنُوْنَ . وَإِذَا قُرِئَ عَلَيْهِمُ الْقُرْآنُ لَا يَسْجُدُوْنَ . بَلِ الَّذِيْنَ كَفَرُوْا يُكَذِّبُوْنَ . وَاللهُ أَعْلَمُ بِمَا يُوْعُوْنَ . فَبَشِّرْهُمْ بِعَذَابٍ أَلِيْمٍ . إِلَّا الَّذِيْنَ آمَنُوْا وَعَمِلُوا الصَّالِحَاتِ لَهُمْ أَجْرٌ غَيْرُ مَمْنُوْنٍ

16. I swear by the twilight,
17. and by the night and by what the night encompasses.
18. By the moon when it is full,
19. you will certainly proceed from phase to phase.
20. What is the matter with them that they do not believe
21. and when the Qur'ān is recited unto them they prostrate not?
22. Rather, the disbelievers (choose to) deny.
23. Allāh is well aware of whatever they amass.
24. So give them the tidings of a painful punishment,

25. except for those who believe and carry out good deeds, theirs shall be an unending reward.

Allāh's ﷻ Great Creation
Verses 16-18

فَلَا أُقْسِمُ بِالشَّفَقِ . وَاللَّيْلِ وَمَا وَسَقَ . وَالْقَمَرِ إِذَا اتَّسَقَ

I swear by the twilight, and by the night and by what the night encompasses. By the moon when it is full,

Allāh ﷻ takes an oath by several phenomena in these verses namely, the twilight, the night and whatever uses the night to rest and the moon when it is full. Allāh ﷻ takes all these oaths to assert that men will certainly proceed from one phase to another in his existence, with each phase becoming severer than the previous one. From this world, man proceeds to the realms of 'Barzakh' (the life of the grave) and then towards Qiyāmah and many stages of the Hereafter.

Sayyidunā Ali ؓ and Sayyidunā Abdullāh Ibn Abbās ؓ and many other eminent Companions ؓ have said that the word Shafaq is the redness in the sky. It is reported from Sayyidunā Abū Hurairah ؓ that Shafaq is the whiteness. Majority of the scholars state that Shafaq is the remaining light of the sun and its redness of the beginning of the night until it is close to the night itself (darkness). Ikrimah's ؓ statement is also similar to this where he stated, 'Shafaq is what is between Maghrib and Ishā Salāh'.

In Sahīh Muslim, it is recorded from Sayyidunā Abdullāh Ibn Amr ؓ that the Holy Prophet ﷺ said, 'The time of Maghrib is as long as Shafaq has not disappeared.' (Muslim)

Imām Shāfi'ī ﷺ and the Sāhibain (Imām Abū Yūsuf ﷺ and Imām Muhammad ﷺ) interpret it to the redness in the horizon and until it remains, the time of Maghrib will remain.

There is an opinion of Imām Abū Hanīfah ﷺ that it refers to the whiteness which appears after the redness but most authentic view is that he has withdrawn from this opinion and taken the first view.

"By the night and by what the night encompasses."

Regarding this verse, Qatādah ﷺ states that it refers to the stars and animals it gathers. Ikrimah ﷺ says, it means, 'What it drives in' due to its darkness, because when it is night time, everything retreats into their dwellings.

The night gathers everyone to take shelter in their respective resting places. As it is observed in our daily lives that all the creation of Allāh ﷻ come out from their homes in search of work, food, luxury etc but soon as the night sets in, everyone returns to their resting places. Here we see all the secret talk, private meetings, illicit affairs, all taking place at night.

According to the Hadīth, it mentions that as soon as night enters, there become three types of people. One group are those who immediately go to sleep after Ishā - for them there is no sin or reward. The second group are those who engage in the worship of Allāh ※, hence they reap their reward from their Merciful Lord and the third group is the one who engage themselves in the disobedience of their Lord, hence perpetrating sins.

"And by the moon when it is full."

Regarding this verse, Sayyidunā Abdullāh Ibn Abbās ※ said, "When it comes together and becomes complete." Qatādah ※ said, "When it completes its cycle." These statements refer to its light when it is completed and becomes full, as the idea was initiated with the night and what it gathers.

Shāh Abdul Azīz ※ mentions in Tafsīr Azīzi that these three oaths signify what will happen to everyone after death. Firstly, the setting of the moon indicates a man's first stage of the grave after the Rūh has been extracted from his body. The Rūh in this juncture has some connection with the world similar to the night which is still connected at that point with the brightness of the day. To this extent it mentions in the Hadīth that a person who was punctual in his Salāh will say, 'Give me a break so I can perform my Salāh'.

Furthermore, it mentions that a person is anxiously waiting for Sadaqah and Isāle-Thawāb to reach him all the time as he is like a person who is drowning in the middle of the ocean.

Secondly, a person reaches the state of disconnecting himself from the Dunya (world) and he now witnesses the results of his own deeds. If they are good, then there is happiness otherwise he suffers constant grief and sorrow. This is indicated by the second oath, **"By the night and what it encompasses."**

Thirdly, the last stage is when after the book of records have been given to each person then everything becomes manifested like the full moon on the fourteenth night whether he has succeeded or not.

Verses 19

لَتَرْكَبُنَّ طَبَقًا عَنْ طَبَقٍ . فَمَا لَهُمْ لَا يُؤْمِنُوْنَ

You will certainly proceed from phase to phase.

Sayyidunā Jābir Ibn Abdullāh ؓ narrates that the Holy Prophet ﷺ said, "These verses remind the person the carelessness of his own creation, the different stages of his life and instructs him to reconsider his position and the consequences (of his attitude in this life as there is still time) and to prepare for the next life."

Ikrimah ؓ said, "from stage to stage means weaned after he was breast fed, and an old man after he was a young man." Hasan Al-Basri ؓ said it means ease after difficulty, difficulty after ease, wealth after poverty, poverty after wealth, health after sickness, and sickness after health."

Allāh ﷻ so eloquently explains the different stages every human being goes through in life in the following verse of Sūrah Hadīd.

اِعْلَمُوْا أَنَّمَا الْحَيَاةُ الدُّنْيَا لَعِبٌ وَّلَهُوٌ وَّزِينَةٌ وَّتَفَاخُرٌ بَيْنَكُمْ وَتَكَاثُرٌ فِي الْأَمْوَالِ وَالْأَوْلَادِ كَمَثَلِ غَيْثٍ أَعْجَبَ الْكُفَّارَ نَبَاتُه ثُمَّ يَهِيجُ فَتَرَاهُ مُصْفَرًّا ثُمَّ يَكُوْنُ حُطَامًا

"Know that the life of this world is merely play (sport), futility (of little use), decoration (superficial), boasting among each other and rivalry (competition) in wealth and children. The example of this is like rain which feeds the plants that amaze (satisfies) the farmers. Thereafter it dries and you will see it become yellow, only to be reduced to bits."

The verse says that this life is play and amusement and an adornment. Furthermore, there is pride and arrogance and boasting, competing in amassing wealth and children against others.

One craves for something at one time so much so that he cannot do without it. Soon as he enters the next phase he regrets that he had made a fool of himself in pursuing trivial things. He then pursues the next phase for different types of desires. When this phase also passes away he gets infatuated with a third desire. All the way through he glances into the past phases and he laughs and trivialises his previous madness and foolishness.

Phases of Life

Allāh ﷻ reminds us in the above verse in Sūrah Hadīd of the different phases of life; from birth to adulthood. During childhood, he wants to pay. There are two types of playing. One type is the competitive in which there is victory and defeat and the other is non competitive. The infant's play is without purpose. All his pursuits are meaningless. Whatever toy he is given, then that is his world. All his time is devoted to it. If that toy is taken away from him then it is as though he has lost his entire world.

As the child grows, the first toy is no more of interest and ignores it. Now, he turns to such play and amusement that seem to have a meaning. It is competitive so he may win or lose. He devotes and dedicates all his time to it and will not pay heed to anyone who tries to divert his attention elsewhere. Slowly and gradually, he grows into a young man. He looks back at his previous pursuits and cast them away as things of uselessness. Now he wants to turn towards personal adornment. He wants decent clothing of latest fashion and designer wear. From head to toe he is concerned of how he can beautify and adorn his appearance. Till now, he had paid no attention to his appearance but this has become the obsession of the youth today.

Previously, he wasn't too concerned with his clothing whether they were untidy, his hair dishevelled or his looks ugly, but suddenly he has become so meticulous over it. This is the madness of our youth.

It continues from here. He reaches to the age of 40. Now looks and appearance are less important to him and more or less settles down. He develops a new interest of accumulating riches, wealth and making a name and fame. He wants to be in the high post offices earning huge salaries. He now has his own children who play with him and he does not mind if his clothes get dirty then and now. At this stage of life his aim and target is to reach a high position in life.

As he enters old age, his goal is to amass riches and to have many children as possible. He hopes to surpass other people in these matters. Even though in today's climate, people don't want large families , but in the past people took pride in large families with many children. In today's society instead of boasting of many children, parents boast of their sons and daughters pursuing high degrees and qualifications achieved.

Now reflect for a moment of time, that when man progresses from one stage of life to the other, he discards the past interest as waste of time. He may even condemn his previous pursuits that once interested him. He now shows disgust and contempt for these different stages.

After Death

Allāh ﷻ warns us so we realise that upon closing ones eyes for departure from this Dunyā towards the life of the Barzakh (grave), the life of the Hereafter will follow. It is at that moment, the real eyes will open up and face the real consequences of our worldly actions. Everything in this worldly life will become worthless even though man was competing with others in them by unlawful ways. Man is like that child who laughed at his interests in infancy and later frowned at the toy with which he could forsake. Unfortunately, the truth is that our eyes do not look beyond the this world to understand its true reality and that of the Hereafter. This journey will continue towards Qiyāmah and the many stages of the Hereafter. After describing the phases of a man's life, Allāh ﷻ gives the example of the worldly life.

كَمَثَلِ غَيْثٍ أَعْجَبَ الْكُفَّارَ نَبَاتُه ثُمَّ يَهِيجُ فَتَرَاهُ مُصْفَرًّا ثُمَّ يَكُوْنُ حُطَامًا

"The example of this is like rain which feeds the plants that amaze the farmers. Thereafter it dries and you will see it become yellow, only to be reduced to bits." (57:20)

The rain turns the dry land into green with other produces. The fields replenishes with its produce that pleases the farmer. Later on, that field dries up and turns yellow and of no use. This is exactly the same scenario with worldly life. In the beginning everything is beautiful and attractive such as, toys and games, pleasures, boastings, possessions and riches. But when one dies and leaves this temporary abode for the next world, then all these things become useless like dried straws.

Verses 20-23
Allāh ﷻ then asks,

فَمَا لَهُمْ لَا يُؤْمِنُوْنَ . وَإِذَا قُرِئَ عَلَيْهِمُ الْقُرْآنُ لَا يَسْجُدُوْنَ . بَلِ الَّذِيْنَ كَفَرُوْا يُكَذِّبُوْنَ . وَاللّٰهُ أَعْلَمُ بِمَا يُوْعُوْنَ

"What is the matter with them that they do not believe and do not prostrate when the Holy Qur'ān is recited to them? Rather, the disbelievers (choose) to deny. Allāh is well aware of whatever they amass."

Despite being presented with clear proofs and knowing that they are approaching nearer to their deaths, they are still heedless and refuse to submit to the divine knowledge of the Holy Qur'ān. However, they should bear in mind that Allāh ﷻ is well aware of whatever they amass, i.e. Allāh ﷻ knows the Kufr (disbelief), the Shirk (ascribing partners to Allāh ﷻ) and the evil that they bear in their hearts.

Some scholars of Tafsīr state **"Whatever they amass,"** refers to the evil deeds that they accumulate in their records of deeds. Allāh ﷻ is aware of all this and will punish them accordingly.

Sajdah Tilāwat

According to Imām Abū Hanīfah ﷺ, Imām Shāfi'ī ﷺ and Imām Ahmad ﷺ there is a Sajdah after the verse,

وَإِذَا قُرِئَ عَلَيْهِمُ الْقُرْآنُ لَا يَسْجُدُونَ

According to Imām Mālik ﷺ, this verse does not constitute part of the Sajdah verses at all like the case in Sūrah Najm and Sūrah Alaq, hence Sajdah Tilāwat is not required at all. The evidence of the three Imāms are as follows. It is reported in Sahīh Muslim and Nasai that Sayyidunā Abū Hurairah ؓ recited Surāh Inshiqāq and he prostrated during its recitiation. Then when he completed the Salāh, he informed them that the Holy Prophet ﷺ prostrated during its recitation.

In a narration of Bukhāri, Sayyidunā Abū Rāfi ؓ says that he prayed Ishā Salāh with Sayyidunā Abū Hurairah ؓ and he (Abū Hurairah ؓ) recited Surāh Inshiqāq, then he prostrated. So, Sayyidunā Abū Rāfi ؓ asked him what type of prostration it was. Sayyidunā Abū Hurairah ؓ replied, "I prostrated behind Abul Qāsim ﷺ and I will never cease to prostrate during its recitation until I meet him." (Bukhāri)

Verse 24
Allāh ﷻ concludes the Sūrah by warning the disbelievers in His proclamation,

$$\text{فَبَشِّرْهُمْ بِعَذَابٍ أَلِيْمٍ}$$

So give them the tidings of a painful punishment.

Although tidings are generally given of pleasant things, the news of punishment is referred to as "tidings" because the disbelievers anticipated that they would be successful by adhering to Kufr and Shirk.

Paradise is Eternal
Verse 25

إِلَّا الَّذِينَ آمَنُوا وَعَمِلُوا الصَّالِحَاتِ لَهُمْ أَجْرٌ غَيْرُ مَمْنُونٍ

Except for those who believe and carry out good deeds. Theirs shall be an unending reward.

Allāh ﷻ says that a person will be saved from eternal chastisement by sincere repentance, acceptance those who believe Islām and carrying out good deeds.

It is a common mode of the Holy Qur'ān to balance between the people of Hell and people of Paradise. Hence, in the concluding verse Allāh ﷻ makes the exception by stating,

Allāh ﷻ in many verses of the Holy Qur'ān clearly states that the blessings and favours of Paradise will be eternal.

In Surāh Hūd, after mentioning the abode of the fortunate believers, He says,

غَيْرَ مَجْذُوذٍ

"This prize (reward of Jannah) will never end". (11:108)

May Allāh ﷻ save us from the fire of Jahannam and enter us through His grace into Jannah. Amīn.

Sūrah Burūj

The Stars
Revealed in Makkah

بِسْمِ اللهِ الرَّحْمٰنِ الرَّحِيمِ

In the Name of Allāh, the Most Compassionate, the Most Merciful

وَالسَّمَآءِ ذَاتِ الْبُرُوجِ . وَالْيَوْمِ الْمَوْعُوْدِ . وَشَاهِدٍ وَّمَشْهُوْدٍ . قُتِلَ أَصْحَابُ الْأُخْدُوْدِ .

النَّارِ ذَاتِ الْوَقُوْدِ . إِذْ هُمْ عَلَيْهَا قُعُوْدٌ . وَهُمْ عَلَى مَا يَفْعَلُوْنَ بِالْمُؤْمِنِيْنَ شُهُوْدٌ . وَمَا

نَقَمُوْا مِنْهُمْ إِلَّا أَنْ يُّؤْمِنُوْا بِاللهِ الْعَزِيْزِ الْحَمِيْدِ . الَّذِيْ لَهُ مُلْكُ السَّمَاوَاتِ وَالْأَرْضِ

وَاللهُ عَلَى كُلِّ شَيْءٍ شَهِيْدٌ

1. By the heaven holding the big stars.
2. By the promised day!
3. By the day which presents itself and the day when people are presented.
4. Cursed are the people of the trenches,
5. a fire that was ignited
6. when they sat by the trenches
7. and were witnesses to what they did to the believers.
8. They sought no retribution from them (the believers) except that they believed in Allāh, the Mighty, Most worthy of praise.
9. To Whom belongs the dominion of the heavens and the earth, and Allāh is Witness to everything.

The Interpretation of the word Burūj
Verse 1

وَالسَّمَآءِ ذَاتِ الْبُرُوجِ

By the heaven holding the big stars

Allāh ﷻ takes an oath by the heaven and it's Burūj. According to Sayyidūna Abdullāh Ibn Abbās ؓ, Mujāhid ؒ, Dahhāk ؒ, Qatādah ؒ and Suddi ؒ, the word Burūj here refers to the giant stars. Allāh ﷻ says,

تَبَارَكَ الَّذِي جَعَلَ فِي السَّمَآءِ بُرُوجًا وَجَعَلَ فِيهَا سِرَاجًا وَقَمَرًا مُّنِيرًا

"Blessed is He Who has placed in the heaven Burūj (giant stars) and has placed therein a great lamp (the sun), and a moon giving light "(25:61)

Other commentators say that the word Burūj is the plural of Burj which means a large mansion or fortress. The Holy Qur'ān says,

وَلَوْ كُنْتُمْ فِي بُرُوجٍ مُّشَيَّدَةٍ

"Even though you are in the fortified castles" (4:78)

Here, the word Burūj means castles or fortresses. The literal meaning of the word Burj is to become manifest. The word Tabarruj means to display ones beauty as in the verse,

وَلَا تَبَرَّجْنَ تَبَرُّجَ الْجَاهِلِيَّةِ الْأُولَىٰ

"And do not display your beauty as it was previously displayed in the time of ignorance" (33:33)

Hence, these commentators take the word Burūj, in this place to refer to mansions and castles that are reserved in the heavens for the guardian angels.

Ibn Jarīr ﷺ prefers the view that it means the position of the sun and the moon, which are twelve Burūj (locations of the mansions). The sun travels through each one of these Burūj in one month. The moon travels through each one of these Burj in two and a third days which makes a total of twenty-eight positions, and it is hidden for two nights.

Verse 2

وَالْيَوْمِ الْمَوْعُودِ

By the promised day

Under the chapter of the commentary of Sūrah Burūj, Imām Tirmizi ﷺ reports a Hadīth from Sayyidūna Abū Hurairah ﷺ in which the Holy Prophet ﷺ stated that the 'promised day' refers to the Day of Judgement, the day which presents itself refers to the Day of Jumu'ah (Friday) and 'the day which people are presented refers to the Day of Arafah (9th of Dhul-Hijjah).

Excellence of Jumu'ah Day

In a Hadīth of Imām Muslim 🙵, it is related from Sayyidunā Abū Hurairah 🙵 that the Holy Prophet 🙵 said, "The best of days on which the sun rises is Friday. On this day, Ādam 🙵 was created, on it he was admitted to Paradise, on it he was sent out of it (to the earth) and the last hour will occur on Friday." (Muslim, Tirmizi)

In another Hadīth, Sayyidunā Abū Hurairah 🙵 narrates that the Holy Prophet 🙵 said, "On Friday, there is a moment in which if a Muslim asks Allāh 🙵 for anything that is good, He will give it to him." (Bukhāri, Muslim)

Sayyidunā Abū Mūsā 🙵 narrates that he heard the Holy Prophet 🙵 say about the opportune moment of Friday. "It is between the time the Imām sits down (on the pulpit to deliver the sermon) until the end of Salāh" (Muslim)

The question arises when is the golden moment when Du'ās are accepted? It can deduced From the Ahādīth that there is most probably a specific time when Du'ās are accepted but it is un-known like Lailatul-Qadr.

Scholars have enlisted more than forty-five different opinions re-garding this specific time from which the two most authentic opin-ions are:

1.   Between the time when the Imām ascends the pulpit until the completion of Salāh. This has been mentioned in the previous

Hadīth.

2. The time between Asr and Maghrib Salāh. This opinion is supported by a Hadīth narrated by Sayyidunā Anas ﷺ in the Sunan of Tirmizi, that the Holy Prophet ﷺ said, "Search for the moment of acceptance on the Day of Jumu'ah after Asr Salāh until the sunset." (Tirmizi)

In another Hadīth, it mentions that the Holy Prophet ﷺ said, "Indeed, among the most excellent of your days is Friday, on it Ādam ﷺ was created, on it he was taken away (meaning he died), on it the trumpet will be blown and the unconsciousness of all creation will take place. Hence, send Durūd on me on this day in abundance for your Durūd will be presented to me. The Companions ﷺ asked, "How will that be when your body will have decomposed. He replied, "Allāh ﷺ has forbidden the earth to consume the bodies of the Prophets."

The Holy Prophet ﷺ has given glad tidings to a believer who dies on a Friday. He said, "Any Muslim who dies on the day of Friday or the night of Friday is protected by Allāh ﷺ from the trials of the grave." (Ahmad, Tirmizi)

In brief, Allāh ﷺ has taken an oath by four prominent objects:
1. The Heaven that has the great stars.
2. The Day of Judgement.
3. Friday.
4. The Day of Arafah.

The relationship between the object of oath and the subject of oath is that they bear evidence to the Divine Omnipotence and they are proof of reckoning, reward and punishment on the Day of Judgement. Friday and the Day of Arafah (the main day of Hajj is the 9th of Dhul-Hijjah of the Islamic Calendar) are blessed days for the believers to gather and accumulate the treasures for the Hereafter. The subject of oath curses the disbelievers who tortured and burned the Muslims because of their faith who suffered persecution whilst at the same time gives glad tidings to the righteous believers of a blissful reward of Paradise in the Hereafter.

The Story of the People of the Trenches
Verses 4-7

قُتِلَ أَصْحَابُ الْأُخْدُودِ . النَّارِ ذَاتِ الْوَقُودِ . إِذْ هُمْ عَلَيْهَا قُعُودٌ . وَّهُمْ عَلَى مَا يَفْعَلُونَ بِالْمُؤْمِنِينَ شُهُودٌ

Cursed are the people of the trenches, a fire that was ignited when they sat by the trenches, and were witnesses to what they did to the believers.

Allāh ﷻ says about the people of the trenches, "Cursed are the people of the trenches which are heavily fuelled fire, when they sit by the trenches and are witnesses to what they did to the believers".

These verses refer to the disbelievers who filled the trenches with fuel and kindled a raging fire threatening the believers of throwing them into the trenches of burning fire if they don't renounce their

40

faith. Its detailed account has been narrated in Sahīh Muslim discussing the story of the sorcerer, monk and the boy. According to some narrations this boy's name was Abdullāh Ibn Tāmir.

Sayyidunā Suhayl ◈ reports from the Holy Prophet ◈ that once he recounted to the Companions ◈ the story of a king who lived in the past. This king had a magician who would practice sorcery for the king. When his magician became old, he approached the king and requested him to send someone to him so that he could teach him magic. Eager that someone should continue the practice after the old magician, the king sent a boy to take lessons from this magician.

Every time the boy visited to the magician for sorcery lessons, he would pass by a monk. One day, he sat with the monk and discovered of what he used to preach (namely the true teachings of Sayyidunā Īsā ◈). Becoming deeply very impressed by this monk he would always sit with him every time before proceeding to the magician for lessons as well as before returning home. The magician would punish him for always being late and so would his family punish him for arriving home late. When he related this to the monk, he suggested that whenever he feared reproach from the magician, he should excuse himself by saying that his family had delayed him and if he feared reproach from his family members, he should tell them that the magician had delayed him. In this manner, he managed to sit regularly with the monk without suffering punishment.

It once occurred that a large animal blocked the path and prevented the people from passing. When the boy arrived there, he thought to himself that this would be the ideal opportunity to test which of the two; the magician or the monk is on the truth. He picked up a stone and prayed, O' Allāh ﷻ! If the way of the monk is more beloved to you than the way of the magician, then kill this beast with this stone so that people could pass'. Consequently, when he threw the stone at the creature, the stone killed it instantly and people were able to pass by peacefully. When the boy related the incident to the monk, the monk said, "You have now become better than me and have reached the high status that I can see. Now listen, you will now be tested (and put through difficulty). When this happens, do not tell anyone about me."

Thereafter, the boy began curing people who were born blind and those who were born with leprosy through his Du'ā to Allāh ﷻ. When a blind minister of the king heard about the boy, he took many gifts along with him and told the boy that he could have everything if he cured him of his blindness. The boy said, "I cannot cure anyone. Only Allāh ﷻ can cure. However, if you believe in Allāh ﷻ, I will pray to Allāh ﷻ and He will cure you." When the minister complied, Allāh ﷻ restored his sight.

When the minister returned to the king's court, the king asked him who had restored his vision. The minister replied, my Lord has restored my sight." The king asked, "Do you have a Lord besides me?" The minister replied, "Allāh ﷻ is my Lord and your Lord. The king arrested the minster and tortured him until he revealed the name of the person i.e. the boy who taught him who his Lord was.

When the boy was summoned before the king, the king said to him, "Your magic has reached a stage where it can cure the blind and people suffering from leprosy." The boy replied, "I cannot cure anyone. Only Allāh ﷻ can cure." The king then punished him severely until he revealed the identity of the monk. When the monk was summoned before the king, the king ordered him to renounce his religion. When the monk refused, the king ordered for a saw to be brought, made the monk lie down and sawed him in half. The king then turned to the minister and tried forcing him to renounce his faith. When the minister refused, the king then ordered for him to be sawed in two.

When it came to the boy's turn, the king instructed him to renounce his faith also. When he refused, the king surrendered to a few of his men and instructed them to take the boy to the highest point of a mountain and threaten to throw him off. If he renounces his religion then set him free, otherwise, throw him off. As they were climbing the mountain, the boy made a Du'ā, "O' Allāh ﷻ, suffice for me against them in which ever manner You please." Allāh ﷻ then caused the mountains to tremor and all the king's men fell to their deaths and The boy returned to the king alone.

When the king asked where his men were, the boy replied that Allāh ﷻ had protected him from their evil. The king then sent him with another party of men, instructing them to take him by a ship to the middle of the ocean and likewise threaten him. If he renounces his faith then bring him back, Otherwise throw him overboard. The boy again prayed, "O' Allāh ﷻ! Suffice for me against them in which ever manner You please." As he made the Du'ā, the ship capsized and all the king's men were drowned. Again the boy returned alone to the king and when the asked about the men, the boy replied that Allāh ﷻ had sufficed for him and protected him from their evil.

The boy then told the king that he was unable to kill him by any method except one. When the king asked him what the method was, the boy said, "Gather the people on a field and tie me to the trunk of a tree upside down. Then take an arrow from my own quiver, place it in my bow (ready to aim) and say, "In the Name of the Lord of this boy, then shoot the arrow." The boy knew that he was to die so he thought of this method to make his death an invitation to his religion for the people. The king did as he was told. He gathered the people, placed the arrow in the bow and shot it saying, "In the Name of the Lord of this boy."

The arrow struck the boy's chest and died instantly, placing his hands on the point where the arrow hit him. Seeing this, the people cried out, "We believe in the Lord of this boy."

The king's men came to him saying, "What you most feared has happened." The king then instructed his soldiers to dig trenches in the streets of the town and to fill the trenches with fire. When this was done, the king instructed his men to bring every believer to the trenches and to tell them to renounce their faith in Allāh ﷻ. If they refused, they were to be thrown into the fire. When this was done all of the people were thrown into the fire. Eventually, a woman carrying her infant child was brought to the trench, and was extremely hesitant. Allāh 🕮 granted speech to her child who said, "O' mother! Be steadfast, because you are certainly upon the truth."

Imām Tirmizi 🕮 reports the same incident with a few additions. At the beginning, the narration of Tirmizi states that a fortune-teller of the king told him that his kingdom was soon to end and it was this fortune-teller who requested the king to send an intelligent boy to him so that he could teach him his craft. This narration also states that when the masses declared, "We believe in the Lord of this boy," someone told the king, "You were just afraid of opposition from the people, the boy, the monk and the minister, now the entire nation is against you. It was then that the king had the trenches dug and announced, "We will say nothing to those who renounce their faith. However, those who do not renounce will be cast into the trenches of fire. It is reference to this incident that Allāh 🕮 states,

"Cursed are the people of the trenches which are heavily fuelled fire, when they sit by the trenches and were witnesses to what they did to the believers. They found no fault in them (the believers) except that they believed in Allāh the Mighty, Most worthy of praise."

The narration of Tirmizi also states that when the grave of the boy was dug up during the Khilāfat (rule) of Sayyidunā Umar 🕮, his hand was found on his chest exactly how he was martyred Muhammad Ibn Ishāq 🕮, reports that the place where the boy, Abdullāh Ibn Tāmir was buried had to be dug up for some important reason during the time of Sayyidunā Umar 🕮, it was found that the body of Abdullāh Ibn Tāmir was intact, and he was sitting up. Someone moved his hand out from that place and his wound started bleeding. When the hand was placed back in its position, the bleeding stopped. There was a ring in his finger which had the inscription 'Allāhu Rabbī' – "Allāh is my Lord". The governor of Yemen informed Sayyidunā Umar ؓ about this, and he wrote back in reply, "Bury the body back as it was with his finger ring" (Ibn Kathīr)

Imām Ibn Kathīr ؒ has quoted Muqātil ؒ who states that the incident of the trenches took place thrice in history. It occurred in Shām during the reign of the Roman emperor Iltanayūs, in Persia during the reign of the emperor Nebuchadnezzar and in Najrān in Yemen during the reign of the king, Yūsuf Dhūtuwās. He also states that the incident in the Holy Qur'ān in Sūrah Burūj refers to the third that occurred in Najrān. Ibn Kathīr ؒ has also quoted from Ibn Abi Hātim ؒ that the incident occurred during the period of "Fatrah" i.e after the ascension of Sayyidunā Īsā عليه السلام , well before the birth of Rasūlullāh ﷺ.

The Only Crime

وَمَا نَقَمُوا مِنْهُمْ إِلَّا أَنْ يُؤْمِنُوا بِاللهِ الْعَزِيزِ الْحَمِيدِ

"They found no fault in them (the believers) except that they believed in Allāh, the Mighty, Most worthy of praise."

The disbelievers had no real justification in killing the believers who committed no crime whatsoever other than the fact that they believed in Allāh ﷻ. This was an unjustified reason which led to indiscriminate killing of the believers only because they chose to follow their obligatory duty.

Allāh ﷻ says,

الَّذِي لَهُ مُلْكُ السَّمَاوَاتِ وَالْأَرْضِ وَاللَّهُ عَلَى كُلِّ شَيْءٍ شَهِيدٌ

"To Him belongs the dominion of the heavens and the earth, Allāh is witness to everything" (85:09)

The disbelievers who perpetrate such acts against the believers do so to show their strength and power and yet fail to realise that Allāh ﷻ is more powerful than them and watching over their actions carefully. Allāh ﷻ will surely punish them for their actions in this life and in the next, hence, they should never assume that they can get away with what they do. Allāh ﷻ refers to this when he concluded the account by saying, Allāh ﷻ is Witness to everything.

Causing Difficulties to the Believers

إِنَّ الَّذِينَ فَتَنُوا الْمُؤْمِنِينَ وَالْمُؤْمِنَاتِ ثُمَّ لَمْ يَتُوبُوا فَلَهُمْ عَذَابُ جَهَنَّمَ وَلَهُمْ عَذَابُ الْحَرِيقِ . إِنَّ الَّذِينَ آمَنُوا وَعَمِلُوا الصَّالِحَاتِ لَهُمْ جَنَّاتٌ تَجْرِي مِنْ تَحْتِهَا الْأَنْهَارُ ذَلِكَ الْفَوْزُ الْكَبِيرُ

10. Indeed those who harm believing men and believing women and do not repent, for them shall be the punishment of Jahannam and the punishment of burning.

11. Most certainly, those who believe and who carry out good deeds shall have gardens beneath which rivers flow, that is the supreme success.

Here, Allāh ✤ gives a warning to those people who harm the believers. This warning is general and does not specifically apply to the people of the trenches. In another verse of Sūrah Ahzāb, Allāh ✤ says,

$$وَالَّذِينَ يُؤْذُونَ الْمُؤْمِنِينَ وَالْمُؤْمِنَاتِ بِغَيْرِ مَا اكْتَسَبُوا فَقَدِ احْتَمَلُوا بُهْتَانًا وَإِثْمًا مُّبِينًا$$

"Those who harm the believing men and women for no sin on their part will bear the burden of slander and a manifest sin." (33:58)

Allāh ✤ mentions this (repentance) after the incident of the people of the trenches, indicating that He would have even forgiven them if they repented and accepted Him as their Lord. Hasan al-Basri ✤ states, "Look at Allāh's ✤ compassion and benevolence. They killed Allāh's ✤ friends, yet He invites them towards repentance and forgiveness."

Allāh's ✤ Mercy

An astounding verse comes to mind which captures the infinite mercy and love of Allāh ✤ for His bondsmen. He says,

مَا يَفْعَلُ اللهُ بِعَذَابِكُمْ إِنْ شَكَرْتُمْ وَآمَنْتُمْ وَكَانَ اللهُ شَاكِرًا عَلِيمًا

"Why must Allāh punish you if you are grateful (for His favours to you) and have Imān. Allāh is Most Appreciative, All-knowing" (4:147)

This means that Allāh ﷻ never punishes those who express their gratefulness to Him and that He rewards them immensely. May Allāh ﷻ make us from the true believers and amongst the Shākirīn (those who express gratitude to Allāh ﷻ).

Verse 11

Allāh ﷻ then speaks about the pious believers in the next verse. He says,

إِنَّ الَّذِينَ آمَنُوا وَعَمِلُوا الصَّالِحَاتِ لَهُمْ جَنَّاتٌ تَجْرِي مِنْ تَحْتِهَا الْأَنْهَارُ ذَلِكَ الْفَوْزُ الْكَبِيْرُ

Most certainly) those who believe and carry out good deeds, shall have gardens beneath which rivers flow, that is the supreme success.

This verse assures the believers that the difficulties of this world are insignificant because they will cause one to attain the "supreme success" of the Hereafter. Burning in a fire in this world will last for only a very short duration, while the bliss and bounty of Paradise will be perpetual.

In a Hadīth Qudsi, Allāh ﷻ states,

"I have prepared for My pious worshippers such things that no eye has ever seen, no ear has ever heard of and nobody has ever imagined of." (Bukhāri)

Then he recited,

فَلَا تَعْلَمُ نَفْسٌ مَّا أُخْفِيَ لَهُم مِّن قُرَّةِ أَعْيُنٍ جَزَاءً بِمَا كَانُوا يَعْمَلُونَ

"No person knows what is kept hidden for them of joy as a reward for what they used to do" (32:17) (Bukhāri)

إِنَّ بَطْشَ رَبِّكَ لَشَدِيدٌ . إِنَّهُ هُوَ يُبْدِئُ وَيُعِيدُ . وَهُوَ الْغَفُورُ الْوَدُودُ . ذُو الْعَرْشِ الْمَجِيدُ . فَعَّالٌ لِّمَا يُرِيدُ

12. **Indeed, the seizing of your Lord is severe.**
13. **Verily, it is He who creates the first time and will create you again.**
14. **He is the Most Forgiving, All Loving,**
15. **Owner of the Throne, the Majestic,**
16. **and the One Who does as He pleases.**

Allāh's ﷻ Power and Might
Verse 12
Allāh ﷻ says,

إِنَّ بَطْشَ رَبِّكَ لَشَدِيدٌ

Indeed, the seizing of your Lord is severe.

Disbelieving nations should not be fooled when Allāh's ﷻ punishment does not overtake them swiftly. A delay in punishment does not mean that it will not arrive. Allāh ﷻ has appointed a time when they will be punished and when this time arrives, they shall be uprooted completely. Sayyidunā Abū Mūsā Al-Ash'ari ؓ narrates that the Holy Prophet ﷺ said, "Verily the time when He seizes him then He gives no respite and the Holy Prophet ﷺ then recited the verse of Sūrah Hūd, where Allāh ﷻ says,

"Such is the seizing of your Lord when He seizes a town that is oppressive. Indeed, His seizing is painful and severe." (Bukhāri)

In Sūrah Al-Fajr, Allāh ﷻ says,

أَلَمْ تَرَ كَيْفَ فَعَلَ رَبُّكَ بِعَادٍ . إِرَمَ ذَاتِ الْعِمَادِ . الَّتِي لَمْ يُخْلَقْ مِثْلُهَا فِي الْبِلَادِ . وَثَمُوْدَ الَّذِيْنَ جَابُوا الصَّخْرَ بِالْوَادِ . وَفِرْعَوْنَ ذِي الْأَوْتَادِ . الَّذِيْنَ طَغَوْا فِي الْبِلَادِ . فَأَكْثَرُوْا فِيْهَا الْفَسَادَ . فَصَبَّ عَلَيْهِمْ رَبُّكَ سَوْطَ عَذَابٍ . إِنَّ رَبَّكَ لَبِالْمِرْصَادِ .

"Have you not seen how your Lord dealt with Ād (who were destroyed by a terrifying stormy wind, (who were the people (the descendants) of (a person called) Iram and who were people (who had the structure) of pillars? The likes of them (in size and strength) were not created in the lands. (Have you not also seen how your Lord dealt with the nation of) Thamūd who used to carve the rocks of the valley (to make their homes in the mountains?) and (have you not also seen how your (Lord dealt with) Fir'awn, the owner of the stakes, these people transgressed (the laws of Allāh) in the lands and caused tremendous corruption so (because of this) your Lord rained punishment on them. Verily, your Lord is Ever Vigilant (and nothing escapes

His attention)." (89:6-12)

Allāh ﷻ is very severe in His punishment when it arrives in it its appointed time. In Sūrah Ankabūt, He says,

فَكُلًّا أَخَذْنَا بِذَنْبِهِ فَمِنْهُم مَّنْ أَرْسَلْنَا عَلَيْهِ حَاصِبًا وَّمِنْهُم مَّنْ أَخَذَتْهُ الصَّيْحَةُ وَمِنْهُم مَّنْ خَسَفْنَا بِهِ الْأَرْضَ وَمِنْهُم مَّنْ أَغْرَقْنَا وَمَا كَانَ اللهُ لِيَظْلِمَهُمْ وَلَكِن كَانُوا أَنفُسَهُمْ يَظْلِمُونَ

"We seized (punished) each of them on account of his sin. Amongst them (were) those, We sent a violent wind (pebble and storm to destroy them like the people of Lūt), some of them (the nation of Thamūd) were seized (destroyed) by a scream, some of them (Qārūn) we swallowed by the ground and some we drowned (Fir 'awn and his army). Allāh was never one to suppress them (by punishing them without first sending guidance to them), but they used to oppress (wrong) themselves (by refusing to accept the guidance that came to them)." (29:40)

Allāh's ﷻ Power to Resurrect
Verse 13

إِنَّهُ هُوَ يُبْدِئُ وَيُعِيدُ

"Verily, it is He who creates the first time and then creates again"

This verse makes it clear to those who deny the Day of Judgement that just as Allāh ﷻ has the power to create people the first time, He is perfectly capable of resurrecting them on the Day of Judgement. It is therefore foolish to regard the Day of Judgement as something farfetched. In Sūrah Ambiyā, Allāh ﷻ says,

كَمَا بَدَأْنَا أَوَّلَ خَلْقٍ نُعِيدُه وَعْدًا عَلَيْنَا إِنَّا كُنَّا فَاعِلِينَ

"Just like we originated the first creation, we shall repeat it reappearing as they had appeared when they were first created) this is a binding (definite) promise upon Us. We are verily the Ones who can do it (Who have the power to fulfil this promise)." (21:104)

Allāh's ﷻ Kindness
Verses 14-16

وَهُوَ الْغَفُورُ الْوَدُودُ . ذُو الْعَرْشِ الْمَجِيدُ . فَعَّالٌ لِمَا يُرِيدُ

He is the Most Forgiving, All Loving Owner of the throne, the Majestic and the One Who does as He pleases.

These verses explain that nothing can stop Allāh ﷻ from doing whatever He wills. He is at liberty to forgive the sinners, to express His love for His pious bondsmen and to punish the disbelievers! Nothing is difficult for Allāh ﷻ, after forgiving the sins of His bondsmen; He starts to love them by showering His infinite mercy upon them. How Merciful Allāh ﷻ is that immediately a person from being a big sinner transforms to become a close friend of Allāh ﷻ. In Sūrah Hajj, Allāh ﷻ says,

إِنَّ اللهَ يُدْخِلُ الَّذِيْنَ آمَنُوْا وَعَمِلُوا الصَّالِحَاتِ جَنَّاتٍ تَجْرِيْ مِنْ تَحْتِهَا الْأَنْهَارُ إِنَّ اللهَ يَفْعَلُ مَا يُرِيْدُ

"Allāh will certainly admit those who believe and perform good deeds into the gardens beneath which rivers flow. Verily, Allāh does as He pleases." (22:14)

Further on after a few verses, He states, **there is none to honour the person whom Allāh humiliates. Indeed, Allāh does as He pleases." (22:13)**

How strongly Allāh ﷻ says,

لَا يُسْأَلُ عَمَّا يَفْعَلُ وَهُمْ يُسْأَلُوْنَ

"He (Allāh) will not be questioned about what He does (because He is above all and everything He does is perfect, most appropriate and above questioning) but they (the people) will be questioned (about the actions they carry out in this world). (21:23)

هَلْ أَتَاكَ حَدِيْثُ الْجُنُوْدِ . فِرْعَوْنَ وَثَمُوْدَ . بَلِ الَّذِيْنَ كَفَرُوْا فِيْ تَكْذِيْبٍ . وَاللهُ مِنْ وَّرَآئِهِمْ مُحِيْطٌ . بَلْ هُوَ قُرْآنٌ مَّجِيْدٌ . فِيْ لَوْحٍ مَّحْفُوْظٍ

17. Has the news of the enemies reached you,
18. of Fir 'awn and Thamūd?
19. Rather the disbelievers are (persistent) in denial,
20. whereas Allāh encompasses them from all over.
21. It is the Glorious Qur'ān
22. in the Preserved Tablet.

In these verses, Allāh ﷻ poses a rhetorical question to warn mankind against adopting the ways of the previously destroyed people such as Fir 'awn and the nation of Thamūd. Instead of accepting the message of Allāh's ﷻ Messengers, these people were haughty and chose to deny 'Tawhīd' (monotheism) and the message of the Prophets ﷺ. Such people should never think that Allāh ﷻ is unaware of their deeds because Allāh ﷻ encompasses them from all directions. Allāh ﷻ knows every misdeed that they commit and will punish them for it as He punished those before them.

Allāh ﷻ warns mankind that the previous nations were destroyed who were much more mightier and powerful than you. How eloquently Allāh ﷻ says,

وَكَذَّبَ الَّذِينَ مِن قَبْلِهِمْ وَمَا بَلَغُوا مِعْشَارَ مَا آتَيْنَاهُمْ فَكَذَّبُوا رُسُلِي فَكَيْفَ كَانَ نَكِيرِ

"Those before them neglected (their Messengers). These people (the polytheist of Makkah cannot ever reach a tenth of what We gave them (the nations of the past), yet they (dare to reject My Messengers), How (grievous) will be My retribution." (34:45)

Glorious Qur'ān
Verses 21-22

بَلْ هُوَ قُرْآنٌ مَّجِيدٌ . فِي لَوْحٍ مَّحْفُوظٍ

It is the Glorious Qur'ān in the Preserved Tablet.

The disbelievers even deny the truth of the Holy Qur'ān. This is only because of their stubbornness, since it is impossible to reject the Holy Qur'ān on reasonable grounds.

The Holy Qur'ān is eternally preserved in the Preserved Tablet, in the heavens and it cannot be altered.

Allāh ﷻ speaks about the authority of His Book in many places in the Holy Qur'ān.

In Sūrah Wāqi'ah, Allāh ﷻ says,

إِنَّهُ لَقُرْآنٌ كَرِيمٌ . فِى كِتَابٍ مَّكْنُونٍ . لَا يَمَسُّهُ إِلَّا الْمُطَهَّرُونَ . تَنْزِيلٌ مِّنْ رَبِّ الْعَالَمِينَ

"Verily this (Revelation to the Holy Prophet) is the honourable Qur'ān (which is recorded) in a preserved book (the Lawhul Mahfūdh). Only the pure ones may touch it. The devils and all evil forces have absolutely no access to it. This Qur'ān is (a Revelation) from the Lord of the universe." (56:77-80)

In Sūrah Hāqqah, He says,

إِنَّهُ لَقَوْلُ رَسُولٍ كَرِيمٍ . وَمَا هُوَ بِقَوْلِ شَاعِرٍ قَلِيلًا مَّا تُؤْمِنُونَ . وَلَا بِقَوْلِ كَاهِنٍ قَلِيلًا مَّا تَذَكَّرُونَ . تَنْزِيلٌ مِّنْ رَبِّ الْعَالَمِينَ . وَلَوْ تَقَوَّلَ عَلَيْنَا بَعْضَ الْأَقَاوِيلِ . لَأَخَذْنَا مِنْهُ بِالْيَمِينِ . ثُمَّ لَقَطَعْنَا مِنْهُ الْوَتِينَ . فَمَا مِنْكُمْ مِنْ أَحَدٍ عَنْهُ حَاجِزِينَ . وَإِنَّهُ لَتَذْكِرَةٌ لِلْمُتَّقِينَ

"Verily this Holy Qur'ān is a word brought (to the Holy Prophet) by an honoured Messenger (Jibrīl) it is not the speech of a fortune-teller, (Despite knowing this) a few are those of you who ponder. It is a Revelation from the Lord of the universe, if he (the Holy Prophet) were to (falsely) attribute some words to us (ascribe to Allāh, words that Allāh had not revealed). We (shall not allow him to go unpunished and We) would seize him by the right hand. We shall then severe (cut) his jugular vein. and none of you will be able to protect (defend) him. (However, since nothing like this happens, it proves that the Holy Prophet propagated truly the message of Allāh). It (The Holy Qur'ān) is certainly advice for those with Taqwa (piety)". (69:40-48)

Allāh ﷻ the challenges mankind when He says,

أَفَلَا يَتَدَبَّرُونَ الْقُرْآنَ وَلَوْ كَانَ مِنْ عِنْدِ غَيْرِ اللهِ لَوَجَدُوا فِيهِ اخْتِلَافًا كَثِيرًا

"Do they not ponder over the Holy Qur'ān? If it were from any other besides Allāh, they would have certainly found many contradictions in it." (4:82)

Allāh ﷻ Himself has taken the responsibility of protecting the Holy Qur'ān He proclaims,

إِنَّا نَحْنُ نَزَّلْنَا الذِّكْرَ وَإِنَّا لَهُ لَحَافِظُونَ

"Without doubt, only We have revealed the Reminder (the Qur'ān) and We shall certainly be its Protectors (ensuring that it remains unchanged throughout time)." (15:19)

Sūrah Tāriq

The Night

Revealed in Makkah

بِسْمِ اللّٰهِ الرَّحْمٰنِ الرَّحِيْمِ

In the Name of Allāh, the Most Compassionate, the Most Merciful

وَالسَّمَآءِ وَالطَّارِقِ . وَمَآ أَدْرَاكَ مَا الطَّارِقُ . النَّجْمُ الثَّاقِبُ . إِنْ كُلُّ نَفْسٍ لَّمَّا عَلَيْهَا حَافِظٌ

1. By the oath of the sky and by that which appears by night.
2. How will you know what it is that appears by night?
3. It is the bright star.
4. There is no soul without a watcher (an Angel) appointed over it (to keep record of all its actions).

Virtues of Sūrah Tāriq

Imām Nasai ﷺ narrates that Sayyidunā Jābir ﷺ said, "Mu'ādh ﷺ lead the Magrib Salāh and he recited Sūrah Al-Baqarah and Sūrah An-Nisā. So, the Holy Prophet ﷺ reprimanded him with the following words,

اَفَتَّانٌ اَنْتَ يَا مُعَاذُ؟ مَا كَانَ يَكْفِيكَ اَنْ تَقْرَءَ وَالسَّمَآءِ وَالطَّارِقِ وَالشَّمْسِ وَضُحَاهَا وَنَحْوِهَا

Are you putting the people in trial, O' Mu'ādh? Was it not sufficient for you to recite Sūrah Tāriq, Sūrah Ash-Shams and Sūrahs similar to them."

Bright Star
Verse 1

وَالسَّمَآءِ وَالطَّارِقِ

By the oath of the sky and by that which appears by night

Sūrah Tāriq is a Makki Sūrah consisting of seventeen verses. In the
opening verses, Allāh ﷻ takes an oath by the sky and by the bright
star to assert that He has appointed an angel to watch over every
person. The work of these angels is to record every deed that a person carries out. Their records of deeds will be presented to them
on the Day of Judgement wherein Allāh ﷻ will decide every person's affair.

Qatādah ﷺ and other scholars say, 'The star has been named Tāriq
because it is only seen at night and it is hidden during the day. His
view has been supported by what has been mentioned in the authentic Hadīth that prohibits a man to come to his family– Tarūq.
This means that he comes to them unexpectedly at night time.

Verses 2-3
Allāh ﷻ first poses a question,

وَمَا أَدْرَاكَ مَا الطَّارِقُ

How will you know what it is that appears by night?

He then answers it Himself,

النَّجْمُ الثَّاقِبُ

It is the bright star.

The word, اَلنَّجْمُ - (Najm) means star. The Holy Qur'ān does not specify any particular star. Therefore, it may be applied to any star. Some of the commentators say that Najm refers to the Pleiades or Saturn and they quote specimens of Arabic speech to confirm their opinion. The word, الثَّاقِبُ (Sāqib) means piercing brightness.

Kirāman Kātibīn
Verse 4

إِن كُلُّ نَفْسٍ لَّمَّا عَلَيْهَا حَافِظٌ

There is no soul without a watcher (an angel) appointed over it (to keep record of all its actions).

This is the subject of the oath, the particle, إِن at the beginning of the verse is used as a negative particle which means 'no' and the particle لَّمَّا (Lammā) is used for exemption here which would mean 'but/except' in the dialect of the grammarians, of Banū Hudhail.

The verse means that there is not a single person over whom there is not a watcher (Hāfiz), which suggests that there is guardian who watches over our actions and deeds so that the reckoning is made on that basis. The word Hāfiz could also mean one who protects someone from calamities. In the first instance, the word Hāfiz refers to the angels who record the deeds. The word Hāfiz although it appears in the singular form, it is used in the general and plural sense, because there is not just one angel recording our deeds but many as indicated in another verse.

$$\text{وَإِنَّ عَلَيْكُمْ لَحَافِظِينَ . كِرَامًا كَاتِبِينَ}$$

"Verily, there are guardians (angels) upon you (with every person), who are noble and are recording." (82:10-11)

The second meaning of the word Hāfiz refers to the angels who have been appointed to protect man from all kinds of calamities that would have befallen him day and night, except the calamities that Allāh ﷻ has decreed for him. Allāh ﷻ states,

$$\text{لَهُ مُعَقِّبَاتٌ مِّنْ بَيْنِ يَدَيْهِ وَمِنْ خَلْفِهِ يَحْفَظُونَهُ مِنْ أَمْرِ اللّٰهِ}$$

"For him (everyone), there are (shift-changing) angels before him and behind him, protecting him under the command of Allāh." (13:11)

Sayyidunā Abū Hurairah ؓ narrates that the Holy Prophet ﷺ said, "Angels come to you in succession by night and day and they all come together at the time of Fajr and Asr Salāh. Then those who stayed with you overnight, ascend (at Fajr) unto Allāh ﷻ, Who asks them and He knows the answer better than they do, "How have you left My slaves?" They reply, "We left them while they were offering (Fajr) Salāh and we came to them while they were offering (Asr) Salāh."

Imām Qurtubi ؒ has reported a Hadīth Mufti Muhammad Shafī Sāhib ؒ mentions in his Ma'āriful Qur'ān that Allāh ﷻ has ap-

61

pointed three hundred and sixty angels for every believer. They protect every limb of his. Of the three hundred and sixty, seven angels alone protect man's ego. These angels defend man from every calamity that is not decreed like a fan chases away the flies coming to a vessel containing honey. If there are no security guards for men, the devils would have snatched them away."

فَلْيَنْظُرِ الْإِنْسَانُ مِمَّ خُلِقَ . خُلِقَ مِنْ مَّاءٍ دَافِقٍ . يَّخْرُجُ مِنْ بَيْنِ الصُّلْبِ وَالتَّرَآئِبِ . إِنَّه عَلَى رَجْعِه لَقَادِرٌ

5. (If man doubts the coming of Qiyāmah), he should think about what he was created from.

6. He was created from spurting water (semen)

7. which emerges from between the backbone and the chest. (This is a reference to men's loins and women's chests)

8. Verily (just as Allāh had the power to create man from nothing) Allāh (also) has the power to return him (on the Day of Qiyāmah).

These verses are alerting man to the weakness of his origin from which he was created. The intent of it is to guide man to accept (the reality of) the Hereafter, because whoever is able to begin the creation is able to repeat it in the same way. How aptly Allāh ﷻ says,

وَهُوَ الَّذِي يَبْدَأُ الْخَلْقَ ثُمَّ يُعِيدُه وَهُوَ أَهْوَنُ عَلَيْهِ

"And it is He Who originates the creation, then He will repeat it and this will be easy for him." (30:27)

The drop of semen is referred to as lowly water in Sūrah Sajdah. Allāh ﷻ says,

$$\text{ثُمَّ جَعَلَ نَسْلَهُ مِنْ سُلَالَةٍ مِّنْ مَّآءٍ مَّهِينٍ}$$

"He then made man's progeny (the generations after Sayyidunā Ādam) from a product of lowly water (sperm)." (32:8)

Allāh ﷻ says in Sūrah Qiyāmah,

$$\text{أَلَمْ يَكُ نُطْفَةً مِّن مَّنِيٍّ يُمْنَى . ثُمَّ كَانَ عَلَقَةً فَخَلَقَ فَسَوَّى . فَجَعَلَ مِنْهُ الزَّوْجَيْنِ الذَّكَرَ}$$
$$\text{وَالْأُنْثَى . أَلَيْسَ ذَلِكَ بِقَادِرٍ عَلَى أَنْ يُحْيِيَ الْمَوْتَى}$$

"Was he (man) not a discharge of semen after which he developed into a clot of blood and then Allāh created him and perfected him? Then Allāh made from it the couple male and female. Does He then not have the power to resurrect the dead?"
(75:37-40)

Creation of Man

Allāh ﷻ describes the semen as spurting water which emerges from between the backbone of men and the chest of women. However, the research of embryological science on this subject shows that the seminal fluid comes out from every part of the human body and every part of the foetus is made of the seminal fluid that has come out from the man's and woman's body. The brain usually plugs the greatest role in this matter. Thus, experience shows that people who indulge in excessive intercourse mostly suffer from mental weakness.

The embryologists have at the same time discovered that the seminal fluid separates from all parts of the body and through the spinal cord, collects in the testicles and from there, it spurts.

They also assert that the brain plays the most important role in the preparation of seminal fluid. The representative of the brain is the spinal cord that has come into the backbone from the brain up to the loins and the testicles. Some of its branches have come into the chest-bones. It is likely that the seminal fluid coming from the chest-bones into the woman's seminal fluid and the seminal fluid coming from the back into the man's seminal fluid have a greater role to play. (Baidhāwi)

A closer observation at the verse, we will notice that it does not specify man or woman. It merely says,

$$خُلِقَ مِنْ مَّاءٍ دَافِقٍ . يَخْرُجُ مِنْ بَيْنِ الصُّلْبِ وَالتَّرَائِبِ$$

He was created from spurting water (semen)

This signifies that the seminal fluid comes out from the entire body of both men and women. The entire body is understood from the mention of the principal organs of the front and back. The front part of the body is the chest and the back part of the body is the loin (back spine).

The expression, 'spurting water,' which emerges from the back and the chest will mean that it comes out from the entire body. Although a child is conceived when the male and female gamete's meet, the verse uses the word, 'water' in the singular sense. Hakīmul Ummah, Shaykh Ashraf Ali Thānwi ﷺ mentions in his masterpiece, Bayānul Qur'ān that the singular form is used because the verse refers to zygote i.e. the cell formed after the union of the male and female gametes.

In the Hadīth, it mentions that women also discharge a form of semen like men. In fact, the Holy Prophet ﷺ mentioned that if the wife's (quantity of) semen is more than that of the husband when they cohabit, the child will resemble the wife's family. If the husband's (quantity of) semen is more, the child will resemble his family. (Muslim)

Verse 8

إِنَّهُ عَلَىٰ رَجْعِهِ لَقَادِرٌ

"Surely, He is Powerful to bring him back." (86:8)

The word, (Raja'a) means to 'bring back' or 'return'. The verse signifies that Allāh ﷺ Who has erected him from a drop of seminal fluid is capable to bring him back to life after death.

How beautifully Allāh ﷺ reminds mankind of his origin in Sūrah Dahr.

هَلْ أَتَىٰ عَلَى الْإِنْسَانِ حِينٌ مِنَ الدَّهْرِ لَمْ يَكُنْ شَيْئًا مَذْكُورًا ۚ إِنَّا خَلَقْنَا الْإِنْسَانَ مِنْ نُطْفَةٍ أَمْشَاجٍ نَبْتَلِيهِ فَجَعَلْنَاهُ سَمِيعًا بَصِيرًا

"Was there a moment in time upon a man when he was (once) something not even worth mentioning (he was still a drop of sperm). Indeed, We have created man from a mixed seed (fusion between the male sperm and female egg) to test him (by prescribing various duties for him) and We made him (a) hearing and seeing being." (76:1-2)

يَوْمَ تُبْلَى السَّرَآئِرُ . فَمَالَهُ مِنْ قُوَّةٍ وَّلَا نَاصِرٍ . وَالسَّمَآءِ ذَاتِ الرَّجْعِ . وَالْأَرْضِ ذَاتِ الصَّدْعِ . إِنَّهُ لَقَوْلٌ فَصْلٌ . وَمَا هُوَ بِالْهَزْلِ . إِنَّهُمْ يَكِيدُونَ كَيْدًا . وَأَكِيدُ كَيْدًا . فَمَهِّلِ الْكَافِرِيْنَ أَمْهِلْهُمْ رُوَيْدًا

9. The day when secrets will be assessed.

10. There shall then neither be any power nor assistant for man.

11. By the sky from which rain falls

12. and by the earth which cleaves.

13. It is definitely a decisive speech

14. and it is no joke.

15. They are certainly conniving a plot

16. and I am also planning a plot.

17. Give the disbelievers respite, grant them reprieve for a while.

Man's Deeds
Verse 9

يَوْمَ تُبْلَى السَّرَآئِرُ

The day when secrets will be assessed

The day when secrets will be examined. The word تُبْلَى (Tublā) literally means to test and examine or to assess and السَّرَائِرُ (Sarāir) means secrets. On the Day of Judgement, the secrets will be tested and examined and laid bare. Man's beliefs, his thoughts, his motives and intentions that were hidden in this life and no one knew about them will be revealed in the Hereafter before him.

Likewise, all those deeds and actions which he committed secretly with no one watching him in this world will be revealed to him and scrutinized in front of him on the plain of Resurrection. Sayyidunā Abdullāh Ibn Umar ؓ said that on the Day of Judgement, Allāh ﷻ will disclose the secrets of all human beings. The sign of every good or bad belief and action will be displayed on man's face, in the form of beauty and light or darkness or gloom (depending on each individual's situation. (Qurtubi)

Another Hadīth narrated by Sayyidunā Abdullāh Ibn Umar ؓ mentions that the Holy Prophet ﷺ states, "Every betrayer will have a flag raised for him behind his back and it will be said, "This is the betrayal of so-and-so, the son of so-and-so."(Bukhāri, Muslim)

In Sūrah Kahf, Allāh ﷻ says,

وَوُضِعَ الْكِتَابُ فَتَرَى الْمُجْرِمِينَ مُشْفِقِينَ مِمَّا فِيهِ وَيَقُولُونَ يَا وَيْلَتَنَا مَالِ هَٰذَا الْكِتَابِ لَا
يُغَادِرُ صَغِيرَةً وَّلَا كَبِيرَةً إِلَّا أَحْصَاهَا وَوَجَدُوا مَا عَمِلُوا حَاضِرًا

**"The book shall be placed and you will see the sinners afraid of
what is contained in them. They will say, 'We are destroyed!
What kind of book is that, it does not leave anything small or
large unrecorded? They will find their deeds present." (18:49)**

Allāh's ﷻ Mercy upon the Believers

Whilst writing the Tafsīr of verse 9 of Sūrah Tāriq, despair over-
came me about our sins being exposed in front of everyone until
later I recalled a Hadīth of Bukhāri which shall hopefully give us
all a glimpse of hope.

Sayyidunā Abdullāh Ibn Umar ؓ relates that I heard the Holy
Prophet ﷺ saying, "Allāh ﷻ will bring a believer near Him and
shelter him with His screen and ask him, Did you commit such
and such sins? He will say, 'Yes, my Lord.' Allāh ﷻ will keep on
asking him till he confesses all his sins and he will think that he is
in ruins. Allāh ﷻ will say, I did screen your sins in the world and I
forgive them for you today. And then he will be given the book of
records of his good deeds. Regarding the disbelievers and hypo-
crites (their evil acts will be exposed publicly) and the witness will
say, These are the ones who lied against their Lord. No doubt! the
curse of Allāh ﷻ is on the wrongdoers."

Verse 10

فَمَا لَهُ مِنْ قُوَّةٍ وَّلَا نَاصِرٍ

There shall then neither be any power nor assistant for man.

Man will be totally helpless on the Day of Judgement and none will be able to help him. Allāh ﷻ says,

هُنَالِكَ الْوَلَايَةُ لِلّٰهِ الْحَقِّ هُوَ خَيْرٌ ثَوَابًا وَّخَيْرٌ عُقْبًا

At times like this, assistance (power) is only from Allāh, the True. (18:44)

Verses 11-14

وَالسَّمَآءِ ذَاتِ الرَّجْعِ . وَالْأَرْضِ ذَاتِ الصَّدْعِ . إِنَّهُ لَقَوْلٌ فَصْلٌ . وَمَا هُوَ بِالْهَزْلِ

By the sky from which rain falls, and by the earth which cleaves. It is definitely a decisive speech and it is no joke.

Allāh ﷻ then takes two oaths to assert that the Holy Qur'ān is true indeed and that it effectively differentiates between truth and falsehood. Using these two oaths to strengthen the affirmation, Allāh ﷻ declares,

"It (the Holy Qur'ān) is definitely a decisive speech and it is no joke."

Sayyidunā Ali ؓ says that he heard the Holy Prophet ﷺ saying about the Holy Qur'ān, "It is a book which describes the stories of the past nations and it contains injunctions for the future generations. It is truly a decisive word and it is no joke."

Verses 15-16

Allāh ﷻ then says,

. إِنَّهُمْ يَكِيدُونَ كَيْدًا . وَأَكِيدُ كَيْدًا

**They (the disbelievers) are certainly conniving a plot and I am
also planning a plot.**

The enemies of Islām continuously harassed the Holy Prophet ﷺ
and the Companions ؓ and prevented people from meeting the
Holy Prophet ﷺ. They labelled false allegations against the Holy
Prophet ﷺ that he was insane, mad, magician and he was only nar-
rating fanciful stories of the past.

Allāh ﷻ says, **"and I am also planning a plot."**

Whilst the disbelievers are busy planning to destroy Islām, Allāh
ﷻ is planning against them as well and eventually cause all of their
plots to be in vain.

Allāh ﷻ says,

هُوَ الَّذِيْ أَرْسَلَ رَسُوْلَه بِالْهُدٰى وَدِيْنِ الْحَقِّ لِيُظْهِرَه عَلَى الدِّيْنِ كُلِّه وَلَوْ كَرِهَ الْمُشْرِكُوْنَ

**"It is He (Allāh) Who sent His Messenger with guidance (Qur'ān
and Sunnah) and the true religion (Islām) so that He may make it
dominant over all other religions even though the polytheist de-
test it." (9:33)**

70

Verse 17

فَمَهِّلِ الْكَافِرِينَ أَمْهِلْهُمْ رُوَيْدًا

Give the disbelievers respite, grant them reprieve for a while.

Allāh ﷻ concludes the Sūrah by consoling and reassuring the Holy Prophet ﷺ not to grieve but to give the disbelievers respite, grant them reprieve for a while and not to worry about the injustice and persecution perpetrated by the polytheist that He himself shall soon deal with them. They will certainly be punished in the Hereafter. Nonetheless, punishment in this world can never be ruled out. It then occurred that the polytheist were defeated in the Battle of Badr as well as in the subsequent battles killing all of their major leaders.

Sūrah A'lā

The Most High

Revealed in Makkah

بِسْمِ اللهِ الرَّحْمٰنِ الرَّحِيْمِ

In the Name of Allāh, the Most Compassionate, the Most Merciful

سَبِّحِ اسْمَ رَبِّكَ الْأَعْلَى . الَّذِيْ خَلَقَ فَسَوّٰى . وَالَّذِيْ قَدَّرَ فَهَدٰى . وَالَّذِيْ أَخْرَجَ الْمَرْعٰى . فَجَعَلَهُ غُثَاءً أَحْوٰى. سَنُقْرِئُكَ فَلَا تَنْسٰى . إِلَّا مَا شَآءَ اللهُ إِنَّهُ يَعْلَمُ الْجَهْرَ وَمَا يَخْفٰى

1. Glorify the Name of your Lord, the Most High.
2. Who created and then proportioned it.
3. Who has measured and then guided.
4. and Who brings out the pasture
5. and then makes it dark stubble (a black heap of debris).
6. We shall soon teach you and you will not forget
7. except what Allāh wills. Verily Allāh knows what is apparent and what is hidden.

The Virtues of Sūrah A'lā

Sayyidunā Barā Ibn Āzib ﷺ reports, "The first Companions of the Holy Prophet ﷺ who came to us in Madīnah Munawwarah were Sayyidunā Mus'ab Ibn Umair ﷺ and Sayyidunā Abdullāh Ibn

Umm Makhtūm ☙ and they started teaching us the Holy Qur'ān. Then came Sayyidunā Ammār ☙, Sayyidunā Bilāl ☙ and Say-yidunā Sa'd ☙. Thereafter, Sayyidunā Umar Ibn Khattāb ☙ came along with a batch of twenty men and then, the Holy Prophet ﷺ came. I never saw the people of Madīnah Munawwarah so pleased with anything as they were with his arrival, to the extent that even the little boys and girls were saying, 'This is Allāh's Messenger ﷺ who has come.' He (the Holy Prophet ﷺ) did not come to Madīnah Munawwarah until I had learned Sūrah A'lā and also other similar Sūrahs." (Bukhāri)

In one narration, Sayyidunā Jābir Ibn Abdullāh ☙ narrates that Sayyidunā Mu'ādh Ibn Jabal ☙ used to offer Salāh with the Holy Prophet ﷺ and then go to lead his own people in Salāh. Once, he lead the people in Salāh and recited Sūrah Baqarah. A man left (the row of the people offering Salāh) and performed Salāh separately and went away. When Sayyidunā Mu'ādh ☙ came to know about it, he said, "He (that man) is a hypocrite." Later, that man learned what Sayyidunā Mu'ādh ☙ had said about him so he came to the Holy Prophet ﷺ and said, "O' Rasūlullāh ﷺ! We are people who work with our own hands and irrigate with our camels by night. Mu'ādh lead us in the night Salāh and he recited Sūrah Baqarah, so I offered my Salāh separately and because of that, he accused me of being a hypocrite." The Holy Prophet ﷺ called Sayyidunā Mu'ādh ☙ and said thrice, "Mu'ādh, you are putting people to tri-al! Recite 'Wash-Shams or Sūrah A'lā or the like."

Verse 1

سَبِّحِ اسْمَ رَبِّكَ الْأَعْلَى

Glorify the Name of your Lord, the Most High

Sūrah A'lā begins by commanding man to glorify Allāh's ﷻ Name. Thereafter, the Sūrah mentions Allāh's ﷻ excellent attributes. The first attribute mentioned is that Allāh ﷻ is Al-A'lā (the Exalted). Abū Dāwūd ﷺ reports from Sayyidunā Uqbah Ibn Āmir ﷺ that when the verse,

فَسَبِّحْ بِاسْمِ رَبِّكَ الْعَظِيمِ

"So glorify the Name of your Majestic Lord,"

was revealed, Rasūlullāh ﷺ instructed the Muslims to include the verse in the Ruku (bowing posture in Salāh and thus the Tasbīh of Ruku was prescribed:

سُبْحَانَ رَبِّيَ الْعَظِيمِ

"Glory be to my Majestic Lord."

Thereafter, when the first verse of Sūrah A'lā was revealed commanding, **"Glorify the Name of your Exalted Lord,"** the Holy Prophet ﷺ instructed the Muslims to include this in the Sajdah, and hence, the Tasbīh of Sajdah is:

سُبْحَانَ رَبِّيَ الْأَعْلَى

"Glory be to my Exalted Lord."

74

Imām Ahmad recorded from Sayyidunā Nu'mān Ibn Bashīr that the Holy Prophet recited Sūrah A'lā and Sūrah Ghāshiyah in the two Eid Salāhs. If the Eid Salāh fell on Friday, he would recite them in both Salāhs (Eid and Jumu'ah). This has been recorded by Imām Muslim, Imām Abū Dāwūd, Imām Nasai, Imām Tirmizi and Imām Ibn Mājah.

Imām Ahmad recorded from Sayyidunā Abdullāh Ibn Abbās that whenever the Holy Prophet would recite **"Glorify the Name of your Lord, the Most High"**, he would say, "Glory be to my Exalted Lord."

$$\text{سَبِّحِ اسْمَ رَبِّكَ الْأَعْلَى}$$

Glorify the Name of your Lord, the Most High.

The word Tasbīh means to pronounce the purity and this verse signifies to honour the Name of your Lord. When the Name of Allāh is pronounced, it should be done with utmost humility and respect. His Name should be kept pure and free from anything that is unbecoming of His sublime status. Allāh should be called by the Name He Himself has stated or taught the Holy Prophet. It is not permitted to call Him by any other name.

Ruling Regarding Allāh's Names

There are some names that are exclusively meant for Allāh. Calling human beings or any other creation by those specific names is contrary to the purity of Allāh, hence not permissible.

Nowadays, people are not careful about names like Abdur-Rahmān, Abdur-Razzāq, Abdul-Ghaffār and Abdul-Quddūs. They call the individual bearing these names like Rahmān, Razzāq, Ghaffār, Quddūs and so on, for short. People have got into the habit of shortening such names without realising that the speakers as well as the listeners are committing a sin. People commit this joyless sin, day and night without any reason.

Some commentators interpret that the word 'Ism' in the verse does not mean 'name' here. Instead, they say it is referring to the 'Dhāt' (Being) of Allāh ﷻ. According to the Arabic expression, this interpretation is not unlikely and the Qur'ān has used the word 'Ism' in that sense also.

The Hadīth that instructs us to recite the Tasbīh in Sajdah does not state, "I pronounce the purity of the Name of my Most Exalted Lord", rather it states, "I pronounce the purity of my Most Exalted Lord." This indicates that in this context, Ism is not used in the sense of Name but it refers to the Being of Allāh ﷻ Himself (Qurtubi).

Verses 2-3

$$اَلَّذِيْ خَلَقَ فَسَوّٰى . وَالَّذِيْ قَدَّرَ فَهَدٰى$$

"Who has created and then proportioned it. And Who has measured and then guided."

All these are the attributes of the Most Exalted. The first attribute is 'Khalaqa' which does not simply mean 'to make' or 'to manufacture'. Its meaning has a deeper significance; which is to bring out something from pure, non-existence without seeking help of any pre-existing matter. This is the correct meaning of creating. If something is made with the help of some pre-existing matter, it cannot be called creation in its original sense. This is not within the power of anyone else. Only the perfect power of Allāh ﷻ can bring things into existence whenever He wills without the help of any pre-existing matter.

The second attribute which is connected with 'Takhlīq' (creation) is 'Sawwā'. This word is derived from 'Taswiyah' and it literally means to skilfully craft something with perfection and symmetry. The verse signifies that Allāh ﷻ made everything symmetrical or made it firmly consistent in its several parts; the body structure, shape and size, limbs and organs. Man and every other animal is adapted to the requirements of wisdom. The hands and legs, the tips of the fingers and toes have joints with different types of springy connective tissues that make it possible to bend and fold in different ways. If we contemplate for a moment at the creation of our limbs and organs, its perfection and symmetry astonishes us and sufficient to believe in the infinite wisdom and power of the Creator of the universe.

The third attribute is 'Qaddara' which is derived from 'Taqdīr' and it means to determine, to measure, to balance, to design symmetrically, to decide. The word is used in the last sense here. The verse explains that the things in the world have not been created without purpose. Everything has been created for a specific purpose and has been endowed with natural capabilities enabling it to function properly. This principle does not apply to one specific species alone. All living and non-living things in the universe have been created to carry out a specific function. For instance, we witness the manifestation of the assignments in the sky, stars, lightning, rain, humans, animals, vegetation and minerals.

The fourth attribute of Allāh ﷻ is 'Fa-Hada' (then guided). In other words, the Creator of the universe did not create things and leave them at their own will to perform their particular role as they like. Rather, they are shown the way of how to perform it. As a matter of fact, He guided the entire creation by equipping every creation of His with specific qualities so to function for what it was created. Whether it is the sky or celestial creation, or the earth or the earthly creation, they all possess special abilities.

The Holy Qur'ān states,

قَالَ رَبُّنَا الَّذِي أَعْطَى كُلَّ شَيْءٍ خَلْقَهُ ثُمَّ هَدَى

"Our Lord is He Who gave to each thing its form and nature, then guided it." (20:50)

As a result, since the inception of their creation, the skies, the earth, the stars and planets, mountains and oceans are all performing their specific functions without failure.

Several other interpretations have been given of the verse, **"Who determined and showed the way."**

These are:

- Allāh ﷻ has shown man the good fortune of virtue and the ill fortune of evil.
- Allāh ﷻ has determined the sustenance of every person and shown him the way to earn this sustenance.
- Allāh ﷻ has predetermined the benefits of everything and has taught man how to exploit these.

Verses 4-5

وَالَّذِيْ أَخْرَجَ الْمَرْعٰى . فَجَعَلَهُ غُثَاءً أَحْوٰى

And Who brings out the pasture, and then makes it dark stubble (a black heap of debris)

The Sūrah also describes Allāh ﷻ when it says that it is Allāh ﷻ Who brings out the pasture. The word 'Mar'ā' originally means pasturage or pasture. This is the land that has grass growing upon which animals graze.

The word 'Guthā' refers to stubble and scum borne upon the surface of a torrent. The word 'Ahwā' is derived from the root 'Huwwah' which refers to a kind of black colour that comes upon a dense vegetation. The verse highlights the divine power and wisdom related to herbage and vegetation. He grows the green vegetation, then He gradually turns it into black colour and it loses its freshness. This directs man's attention also to its end. His body radiating with health, beauty, smartness and alertness is a divine gift but its lifespan is limited and eventually it will come to an end.

The Holy Qur'ān
Verses 6-8

سَنُقْرِئُكَ فَلَا تَنْسَى . إِلَّا مَا شَاءَ اللهُ إِنَّهُ يَعْلَمُ الْجَهْرَ وَمَا يَخْفَى

We shall soon teach you and you will not forget. Except what Allāh wills. Verily Allāh knows what is apparent and what is hidden.

Here Allāh ﷻ is addressing the Holy Prophet ﷺ that he will never be made to forget anything revealed to him.

This message is also repeated in Sūrah Qiyāmah where Allāh ﷻ says,

إِنَّ عَلَيْنَا جَمْعَهُ وَقُرْآنَهُ

"Verily, it is Our responsibility to collect it (the Qur'ān) and to make you recite it." (75:17)

While Allāh ﷻ made the Holy Prophet ﷺ remember all of the Qur'ān, there were certain verses which Allāh ﷻ made the Holy Prophet ﷺ forget because they had been abrogated. This was done by Allāh's ﷻ command and it is not without reason.

Allāh ﷻ says in Sūrah Baqarah,

مَا نَنْسَخْ مِنْ آيَةٍ أَوْ نُنْسِهَا نَأْتِ بِخَيْرٍ مِنْهَا أَوْ مِثْلِهَا أَلَمْ تَعْلَمْ أَنَّ اللهَ عَلَى كُلِّ شَيْءٍ قَدِيرٌ

" Whatever We abrogate of any verse or cause it to be forgotten, We bring something better or equivalent to it. Do you not know that Allāh has power over all things?" (2:106)

Some scholars interpret the exceptive sentence, **"except what Allāh wills."** differently. They say that for some reason Allāh ﷻ blotted out temporarily, a verse from the Holy Prophet's ﷺ memory but he may have remembered it again. In support of this, there is a Hadīth in which it says, "One day the Holy Prophet ﷺ recited a Sūrah but omitted one of the verses. Sayyidunā Ubay Ibn Ka'b ﷺ, one of the Holy Prophet's ﷺ scribes was present. He thought it might have been abrogated. On enquiry, the Holy Prophet ﷺ said that it was not abrogated but that it was omitted by mistake (meaning he forgot to read it). (Qurtubi)

In this interpretation, it may be summarised that forgetting a verse temporarily and then, remembering it again, does not go against the promise made in the verse. In fact, it is an exception from this promise. Allāh ﷻ continues,

"Verily, Allāh knows what is apparent and what is hidden."

Allāh ﷻ knows the apparent and inner condition of every person. Nothing is hidden from Him.

وَنُيَسِّرُكَ لِلْيُسْرٰى . فَذَكِّرْ إِنْ نَّفَعَتِ الذِّكْرٰى . سَيَذَّكَّرُ مَنْ يَّخْشٰى . وَيَتَجَنَّبُهَا الْأَشْقَى . الَّذِيْ يَصْلَى النَّارَ الْكُبْرٰى . ثُمَّ لَا يَمُوْتُ فِيْهَا وَلَا يَحْيٰى . قَدْ أَفْلَحَ مَنْ تَزَكّٰى . وَذَكَرَ اسْمَ رَبِّهِ فَصَلّٰى

8.We shall soon make the easy Shari'ah simple for you.
9. So advice if advice is beneficial.

10. The one who fears will take heed.

11. And (only) he will keep away from it who is most unfortunate,

12. and who shall enter the gigantic fire.

13. He will then neither die there nor live.

14. Successful indeed is he who has adopted purity.

15. Who takes the Name of his Lord and performs Salāh.

Practicing Dīn is Easy
Verse 8

وَنُيَسِّرُكَ لِلْيُسْرَى

We shall soon make the easy Shari'ah simple for you

Addressing the Holy Prophet ﷺ further, Allāh ﷻ says, **"We shall
soon make the easy Shari'ah simple for you."** In this verse, Allāh
ﷻ promises the Holy Prophet ﷺ that his Shariah shall be easy to
practise. No injunction of the Shari'ah is beyond man's capability
and no injunction will cause excessive difficulty to a person. If an
ill person cannot stand and perform Ruku and Sajdah, he is allowed to sit and perform the Ruku and Sajdah. If he cannot do this,
he may sit and perform the Ruku and Sajdah by merely lowering
his head. If this is also not possible, he may perform the entire
Salāh while lying down.

Zakāt is due only from the person who possesses money equivalent to Nisāb. When Zakāt does become obligatory for one, it is only 2.5% of one's total wealth that is given (97.5% remains with
him). Then too, Zakāt will be paid only from certain commodities

as opposed to from one's entire wealth e.g. one's necessities will not be added to the total amount when calculating Zakāt. Similarly, Hajj is obligatory only once in a lifetime upon those Muslims who can afford it, otherwise it is not necessary.

As far as the fasting of Ramadhān is concerned, a person who is ill, travelling, expecting, or breastfeeding may omit them and make them up later upon recovery. Among the concessions that the Shari'ah has allowed is that travellers should perform only two Rak'ats Fardh Salāh instead of four. Besides the above, there are numerous other concessions that the Shari'ah allows in various circumstances. The details of these can be found in the books of Islamic jurisprudence.

Verse 9

فَذَكِّرْ إِنْ نَّفَعَتِ الذِّكْرَى

So advice if advice is beneficial.

This verse seems to indicate that advice should be given only when one deems it to be beneficial. The verse contains the conditional particle of 'in' (**if**) that apparently makes the sentence a conditioned statement. But in fact, the command is not intended to be made conditioned. It is rather an emphatic statement. This is similar in many languages. The particle 'if' is sometimes used when something is always true. It is used for introducing a situation that always has the same meaning or results. For example, if you are a man (obviously he is a man), then you will do this work. In neither of such sentences, the particle 'if' is conditioned, but rather emphatic. Likewise, the verse explains that preaching truth and right-eousness is certainly useful. Therefore, any beneficial thing should never be abandoned at anytime.

Fire of Jahannam
Verses 10-13

سَيَذَّكَّرُ مَنْ يَّخْشَى . وَيَتَجَنَّبُهَا الْأَشْقَى . الَّذِيْ يَصْلَى النَّارَ الْكُبْرَى . ثُمَّ لَا يَمُوْتُ فِيْهَا وَلَا يَحْيٰى

The one who fears will take heed whereas only he will keep away from it (from the advice) who is most unfortunate and who shall enter the gigantic fire. He will then neither die there nor live

The fire of Jahannam is described as a gigantic fire because it is seventy times more intense than the fire of this world. Describing the people entering Jahannam, none will die in it because the life of the Ākhirah is eternal. The life of the people in Jahannam can nei-ther be described as life because of the misery they will suffer therein. Allāh ﷻ says in Sūrah Fātir,

وَالَّذِيْنَ كَفَرُوْا لَهُمْ نَارُ جَهَنَّمَ لَا يُقْضَى عَلَيْهِمْ فَيَمُوْتُوْا وَلَا يُخَفَّفُ عَنْهُمْ مِنْ عَذَابِهَا كَذٰلِكَ نَجْزِيْ كُلَّ كَفُوْرٍ

"The Fire of Jahannam will be for those who disbelieve, where no decree will be passed against them so that they may die. Their punishment will also not be lightened. Thus do We punish every disbeliever." (35:35)

In Sūrah Ibrāhīm, Allāh ﷻ says,

وَيَأْتِيهِ الْمَوْتُ مِنْ كُلِّ مَكَانٍ وَّمَا هُوَ بِمَيِّتٍ وَّمِنْ وَّرَائِهِ عَذَابٌ غَلِيْظٌ

"(The causes of) Death will come to him from all sides, but he will not die. Before him will be severe punishment." (14:17)

Verses 14-15

قَدْ أَفْلَحَ مَنْ تَزَكّٰى . وَذَكَرَ اسْمَ رَبِّه فَصَلّٰى

Successful indeed is he who has adopted purity. Who takes the Name of his Lord and performs Salāh

In the above verse, the word, 'Tazakkā' is derived from Zakāh, the primary meaning of which is "to purify". The Zakāt of wealth is so called because it purifies the rest of the man's wealth for him. In this context, the word 'Tazakkā' is used in general sense, which comprehends the purity of faith and character and purity of wealth.

بَلْ تُؤْثِرُوْنَ الْحَيَاةَ الدُّنْيَا . وَالْآخِرَةُ خَيْرٌ وَّأَبْقٰى . إِنَّ هٰذَا لَفِي الصُّحُفِ الْأُوْلَى ,
صُحُفِ إِبْرَاهِيْمَ وَمُوْسٰى

16. However, they prefer the life of this world.
17. Whereas the Hereafter is much better and much more lasting.
18. Undoubtedly, this is in the previous scriptures.
19. The scriptures of Ibrāhīm and Mūsā.

Reality of the World
Verses 16-17

$$\text{بَلْ تُؤْثِرُوْنَ الْحَيَاةَ الدُّنْيَا . وَالْآخِرَةُ خَيْرٌ وَّأَبْقَى}$$

However, they prefer the life of this world. Whereas the Hereafter is much better and much more lasting.

Allāh ﷻ then mentions the reason for man's failure to succeed in the Hereafter. The reason is that 'they prefer the life of this world whereas the Hereafter is much better and much more lasting'. The superiority of the Hereafter over this world is evident from the fact that the reward of a single deed in the Hereafter is better than everything that this world contains.

In Sahīh Bukhāri under the chapter, "The example of this world in contrast with the Hereafter," a Hadīth is quoted,

"A small place equal to an area occupied by a whip in Paradise is better than the (whole) world and whatever is in it; and a journey in the morning or in the evening in the path of Allāh ﷻ is better than the whole world and whatever is in it." (Bukhāri)

How beautifully Sayyidunā Ali ؓ says,

"The world is travelling, turning its back and the Ākhirah is moving, travelling in advance. For each one there are individuals. So therefore, become from the people of the Hereafter and do not become from the people of the Dunya because there is practice today and no account and tomorrow there is account but no practice."

In a Hadīth of Bukhārī, Sayyidunā Abdullāh Ibn Umar ؓ says,

"Allāh's Messenger ﷺ took hold of my shoulder and said, "Be in this world as if you are a stranger or a traveller."

The sub-narrator added, Sayyidunā Abdullāh Ibn Umar ؓ used to say, "If you survive till the evening then do not expect to be alive in the morning, and if you survive till the morning then do not expect to be alive in the evening, and."

In another Hadīth, the Holy Prophet ﷺ says,

"The son of Ādam (i.e. man) grows old and two desires remain young, his love for wealth and (a wish for) a long life." (Bukhārī)

Sayyidunā Abdullāh Ibn Mas'ūd ؓ says that people generally prefer the worldly blessings and comforts to the blessings and comforts of the Hereafter because the former is visible and readily available, while the latter is invisible and presently unavailable. People unaware of reality prefer the visible over the invisible, which becomes the cause of eternal loss.

An intelligent person will never prefer this world over the next because this world is short-lived. How can he give importance to that which will soon pass away from him, while ignoring the importance of the abode of eternity and infinity.

Imām Ahmad ؓ narrates a Hadīth from Sayyidunā Abū Mūsā Al-

Ash'ari ❧ that the Holy Prophet ❧ said,

"Whoever loves his worldly life will suffer in the Hereafter and whoever loves the Hereafter will suffer in his worldly life. Therefore, choose that which is everlasting over that which is temporary." (Ahmad)

Verses 18-19

إِنَّ هٰذَا لَفِي الصُّحُفِ الْأُوْلَى , صُحُفِ إِبْرَاهِيْمَ وَمُوسى

Undoubtedly, this is in the previous scriptures. The scriptures of Ibrāhīm and Mūsā.

In Rūhul-Ma'āni, there is a narration of Sayyidunā Abū Dharr ❧ that he once asked the Holy Prophet ❧ whether anything from the scriptures of Sayyidunā Ibrāhīm عليه السلام and Sayyidunā Mūsā عليه السلام was revealed to him. The Holy Prophet ❧ replied in the affirmative and then recited the verses of this Sūrah from verses 14 to 17.

Sūrah Najm also alludes to the contents of the scriptures given to Sayyidunā Ibrāhīm عليه السلام and Sayyidunā Mūsā عليه السلام. The subject matter begins with verses 36 and 37 of the Sūrah, where Allāh ﷻ says,

أَمْ لَمْ يُنَبَّأْ بِمَا فِيْ صُحُفِ مُوسى. وَإِبْرَاهِيْمَ الَّذِيْ وَفّٰى

"Had he not been informed of what appeared in the scriptures of Mūsā? And in the scriptures of Ibrāhīm who fulfilled." (53:36-37)

<u>Themes of the Script of Sayyiduna Ibrāhīm ﷺ</u>

In Ma'āriful Qur'ān, Mufti Muhammad Shafī Sāhib ﷺ mentions a narration from Sayyidunā Abū Dharr ﷺ that he inquired from the Holy Prophet ﷺ as to the contents of the scripts of Prophet Ibrāhīm ﷺ and the Prophet ﷺ replied that they contained educating parables.

A story is mentioned about a tyrant king where he is addressed and told; You haughty, arrogant and oppressive ruler! I did not give you kingdom so that you may amass wealth, but I had given you power so that you may let the supplication of the oppressed against the oppressor reach Me, because My law does not reject the supplication of an oppressed, even though it may be uttered by a disbeliever.

Another parable addresses the general public; A wise person should divide his time into three parts. One part should be reserved for the worship of his Lord and supplication to Him. The second part should be reserved for self assessment of his deeds and reflection on the omnipotence and creation of Allāh ﷻ. The third part should be allocated for acquisition of livelihood and fulfilling the natural needs.

Themes of the Script of Sayyidunā Mūsā ﷺ

1. I am surprised at the person who believes that he will certainly die and yet he lives happily.

2. I am surprised at the person who believes in divine destiny and yet he is despondent and aggrieved.

3. I am surprised at the person who experiences the reality of life and rise and fall of nations and yet he is content with the world.

4. I am surprised at the person who believes in the reckoning of the Hereafter and yet he abandons good deeds.

Other titles from JKN Publications

Your Questions Answered

An outstanding book written by Shaykh Mufti Saiful Islām. A very comprehensive yet simple Fatāwa book and a source of guidance that reaches out to a wider audience i.e. the English speaking Muslims. The reader will benefit from the various answers to questions based on the Laws of Islām relating to the beliefs of Islām, knowledge, Sunnah, pillars of Islām, marriage, divorce and contemporary issues.

Hadeeth for Beginners

A concise Hadeeth book with various Ahādeeth that relate to basic Ibādāh and moral etiquettes in Islām accessible to a wider readership. Each Hadeeth has been presented with the Arabic text, its translation and commentary to enlighten the reader, its meaning and application in day-to-day life.

UK RRP: £3.00

Du'ā for Beginners

This book contains basic Du'ās which every Muslim should recite on a daily basis. Highly recommended to young children and adults studying at Islamic schools and Madrasahs so that one may cherish the beautiful treasure of supplications of our beloved Prophet ﷺ in one's daily life, which will ultimately bring peace and happiness in both worlds, Inshā-Allāh.

UK RRP: £2.00

How well do you know Islām?

An exciting educational book which contains 300 multiple questions and answers to help you increase your knowledge on Islām! Ideal for the whole family, especially children and adult students to learn new knowledge in an enjoyable way and cherish the treasures of knowledge that you will acquire from this book. A very beneficial tool for educational syllabus.

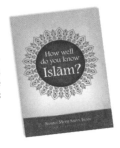

Treasures of the Holy Qur'ān

This book entitled "Treasures of the Holy Qur'ān" has been compiled to create a stronger bond between the Holy Qur'ān and the readers. It mentions the different virtues of Sūrahs and verses from the Holy Qur'ān with the hope that the readers will increase their zeal and enthusiasm to recite and inculcate the teachings of the Holy Qur'ān into their daily lives.

UK RRP: £3.00

Marriage - A Complete Solution

Islām regards marriage as a great act of worship. This book has been designed to provide the fundamental teachings and guidelines of all what relates to the marital life in a simplified English language. It encapsulates in a nutshell all the marriage laws mentioned in many of the main reference books in order to facilitate their understanding and implementation.

UK RRP: £5.00

Pearls of Luqmān

This book is a comprehensive commentary of Sūrah Luqmān, written beautifully by Shaykh Mufti Saiful Islām. It offers the reader with an enquiring mind, abundance of advice, guidance, counselling and wisdom.

The reader will be enlightened by many wonderful topics and anecdotes mentioned in this book, which will create a greater understanding of the Holy Qur'ān and its wisdom. The book highlights some of the wise sayings and words of advice Luqmān ﷺ gave to his son.

UK RRP: £3.00

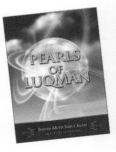

Arabic Grammar for Beginners

This book is a study of Arabic Grammar based on the subject of Nahw (Syntax) in a simplified English format. If a student studies this book thoroughly, he/she will develop a very good foundation in this field, Inshā-Allāh. Many books have been written on this subject in various languages such as Arabic, Persian and Urdu. However, in this day and age there is a growing demand for this subject to be available in English .

UK RRP: £3.00

A Gift to My Youngsters

This treasure filled book, is a collection of Islamic stories, morals and anecdotes from the life of our beloved Prophet ﷺ, his Companions ﷺ and the pious predecessors. The stories and anecdotes are based on moral and ethical values, which the reader will enjoy sharing with their peers, friends, families and loved ones.

"A Gift to My Youngsters" – is a wonderful gift presented to the readers personally, by the author himself, especially with the youngsters in mind. He has carefully selected stories and anecdotes containing beautiful morals, lessons and valuable knowledge and wisdom.

UK RRP: £5.00

Travel Companion

The beauty of this book is that it enables a person on any journey, small or distant or simply at home, to utilise their spare time to read and benefit from an exciting and vast collection of important and interesting Islamic topics and lessons. Written in simple and easy to read text, this book will immensely benefit both the newly interested person in Islām and the inquiring mind of a student expanding upon their existing knowledge. Inspiring reminders from the Holy Qur'ān and the blessed words of our beloved Prophet ﷺ beautifies each topic and will illuminate

Pearls of Wisdom

Junaid Baghdādi ﷺ once said, "Allāh ﷻ strengthens through these Islamic stories the hearts of His friends, as proven from the Qur'anic verse,
"And all that We narrate unto you of the stories of the Messengers, so as to strengthen through it your heart." (11:120)
Mālik Ibn Dinār ﷺ stated that such stories are gifts from Paradise. He also emphasised to narrate these stories as much as possible as they are gems and it is possible that an individual might find a truly rare and invaluable gem among them. **UK RRP: £6.00**

Inspirations

This book contains a compilation of selected speeches delivered by Shaykh Mufti Saiful Islām on a variety of topics such as the Holy Qur'ān, Nikāh and eating Halāl. Having previously been compiled in separate booklets, it was decided that the transcripts be gathered together in one book for the benefit of the reader. In addition to this, we have included in this book, further speeches which have not yet been printed.

UK RRP: £6.00

Gift to my Sisters

A thought provoking compilation of very interesting articles including real life stories of pious predecessors, imaginative illustrations and much more. All designed to influence and motivate mothers, sisters, wives and daughters towards an ideal Islamic lifestyle. A lifestyle referred to by our Creator, Allāh ﷻ in the Holy Qur'ān as the means to salvation and ultimate success.

UK RRP: £6.00

Gift to my Brothers

A thought provoking compilation of very interesting articles including real life stories of pious predecessors, imaginative illustrations, medical advices on intoxicants and rehabilitation and much more. All designed to influence and motivate fathers, brothers, husbands and sons towards an ideal Islamic lifestyle. A lifestyle referred to by our Creator, Allāh ﷻ in the Holy Qur'ān as the means to salvation and ultimate success.

UK RRP: £5.00

Heroes of Islām

"In the narratives there is certainly a lesson for people of intelligence (understanding)." (12:111)

A fine blend of Islamic personalities who have been recognised for leaving a lasting mark in the hearts and minds of people.

A distinguishing feature of this book is that the author has selected not only some of the most world and historically famous renowned scholars but also these lesser known and a few who have simply left behind a valuable piece of advice to their nearest and dearest. **UK RRP: £5.00**

Ask a Mufti (3 volumes)

Muslims in every generation have confronted different kinds of challenges. Inspite of that, Islām produced such luminary Ulamā who confronted and responded to the challenges of their time to guide the Ummah to the straight path.

"Ask A Mufti" is a comprehensive three volume fatwa book, based on the Hanafi School, covering a wide range of topics related to every aspect of human life such as belief, ritual worship, life after death and contemporary legal topics related to purity, commercial transaction, marriage, divorce, food, cosmetic, laws pertaining to women, Islamic medical ethics and much more.

UK RRP: £30.00

Should I Follow a Madhab?

Taqleed or following one of the four legal schools is not a new phenomenon. Historically, scholars of great calibre and luminaries, each one being a specialist in his own right, were known to have adhered to one of the four legal schools. It is only in the previous century that a minority group emerged advocating a severe ban on following one of the four major schools.

This book endeavours to address the topic of Taqleed and elucidates its importance and necessity in this day and age. It will also, by the Divine Will of Allāh ﷻ dispel some of the confusion surrounding this topic. **UK RRP: £5.00**

Advice for the Students of Knowledge

Allāh ﷻ describes divine knowledge in the Holy Qur'ān as a 'Light'. Amongst the qualities of light are purity and guidance. The Holy Prophet ﷺ has clearly explained this concept in many blessed Ahādeeth and has also taught us many supplications in which we ask for beneficial knowledge.

This book is a golden tool for every sincere student of knowledge wishing to mould his/her character and engrain those correct qualities in order to be worthy of receiving the great gift of Ilm from Allāh ﷻ. **UK RRP: £3.00**

Stories for Children

"Stories for Children" - is a wonderful gift presented to the readers personally by the author himself, especially with the young children in mind. The stories are based on moral and ethical values, which the reader will enjoy sharing with their peers, friends, families and loved ones. The aim is to present to the children stories and incidents which contain moral lessons, in order to reform and correct their lives, according to the Holy Qur'ān and Sunnah.

UK RRP: £5.00

Pearls from My Shaykh

This book contains a collection of pearls and inspirational accounts of the Holy Prophet ﷺ, his noble Companions, pious predecessors and some personal accounts and sayings of our well-known contemporary scholar and spiritual guide, Shaykh Mufti Saiful Islām Sāhib. Each anecdote and narrative of the pious predecessors have been written in the way that was narrated by Mufti Saiful Islām Sāhib in his discourses, drawing the specific lessons he intended from telling the story. The accounts from the life of the Shaykh has been compiled by a particular student based on their own experience and personal observation. **UK RRP: £5.00**

Paradise & Hell

This book is a collection of detailed explanation of Paradise and Hell including the state and conditions of its inhabitants. All the details have been taken from various reliable sources. The purpose of its compilation is for the reader to contemplate and appreciate the innumerable favours, rewards, comfort and unlimited luxuries of Paradise and at the same time take heed from the punishment of Hell. Shaykh Mufti Saiful Islām Sāhib has presented this book in a unique format by including the Tafseer and virtues of Sūrah Ar-Rahmān. **UK RRP: £5.00**

Prayers for Forgiveness

Prayers for Forgiveness' is a short compilation of Du'ās in Arabic with English translation and transliteration. This book can be studied after 'Du'ā for Beginners' or as a separate book. It includes twenty more Du'ās which have not been mentioned in the previous Du'ā book. It also includes a section of Du'ās from the Holy Qur'ān and a section from the Ahādeeth. The book concludes with a section mentioning the Ninety-Nine Names of Allāh ﷻ with its translation and transliteration. **UK RRP: £3.00**

Scattered Pearls

This book is a collection of scattered pearls taken from books, magazines, emails and WhatsApp messages. These pearls will hopefully increase our knowledge, wisdom and make us realise the purpose of life. In this book, Mufti Sāhib has included messages sent to him from scholars, friends and colleagues which will be beneficial and interesting for our readers Inshā-Allāh. **UK RRP: £4.00**

Poems of Wisdom

This book is a collection of poems from those who contributed to the Al-Mumin Magazine in the poems section. The Hadeeth mentions "Indeed some form of poems are full of wisdom." The themes of each poem vary between wittiness, thought provocation, moral lessons, emotional to name but a few. The readers will benefit from this immensely and make them ponder over the outlook of life in general.

UK RRP: £4.00

Horrors of Judgement Day
This book is a detailed and informative commentary of the first three Sūrahs of the last Juz namely; Sūrah Naba, Sūrah Nāzi'āt and Sūrah Abasa. These Sūrahs vividly depict the horrific events and scenes of the Great Day in order to warn mankind the end of this world. These Sūrahs are an essential reminder for us all to instil the fear and concern of the Day of Judgement and to detach ourselves from the worldly pleasures. Reading this book allows us to attain the true realization of this world and provides essential advices of how to gain eternal salvation in the Hereafter.

RRP: £5:00

Spiritual Heart
It is necessary that Muslims always strive to better themselves at all times and to free themselves from the destructive maladies. This book focusses on three main spiritual maladies; pride, anger and evil gazes. It explains its root causes and offers some spiritual cures. Many examples from the lives of the pious predecessors are used for inspiration and encouragement for controlling the above three maladies. It is hoped that the purification process of the heart becomes easy once the underlying roots of the above maladies are clearly understood.
UK RRP: £5:00

Hajj & Umrah for Beginners
This book is a step by step guide on Hajj and Umrah for absolute beginners. Many other additional important rulings (Masāil) have been included that will Insha-Allāh prove very useful for our readers. The book also includes some etiquettes of visiting (Ziyārat) of the Holy Prophet's ﷺ blessed Masjid and his Holy Grave.

UK RRP £3:00

Advice for the Spiritual Travellers
This book contains essential guidelines for a spiritual Murīd to gain some familiarity of the science of Tasawwuf. It explains the meaning and aims of Tasawwuf, some understanding around the concept of the soul, and general guidelines for a spiritual Murīd. This is highly recommended book and it is hoped that it gains wider readership among those Murīds who are basically new to the science of Tasawwuf.
UK RRP £3:00

Don't Worry Be Happy
This book is a compilation of sayings and earnest pieces of advice that have been gathered directly from my respected teacher Shaykh Mufti Saiful Islām Sāhib. The book consists of many valuable enlightenments including how to deal with challenges of life, promoting unity, practicing good manners, being optimistic and many other valuable advices. Our respected Shaykh has gathered this Naseehah from meditating, contemplating, analysing and searching for the gems within Qur'anic verses, Ahādeeth and teachings of our Pious Predecessors. **UK RRP £1:00**